TORCH BIBLE
COMMENTARIES

General Editors

THE REV. JOHN MARSH, D.PHIL.
Principal of Mansfield College, Oxford

THE REV. DAVID L. EDWARDS, M.A.
Editor, SCM Press

THE REV. CANON ALAN RICHARDSON, D.D.
Professor of Christian Theology in the University of Nottingham

FOREWORD TO SERIES

The aim of this series of commentaries on books of the Bible is to provide the general reader with the soundest possible assistance in understanding the message of each book considered as a whole and as a part of the Bible.

The findings and views of modern critical scholarship on the text of the Bible have been taken fully into account; but we have asked the writers to remember that the Bible is more than a quarry for the practice of erudition; that it contains the living message of the living God.

We hope that intelligent people of varying interests will find that these commentaries, while not ignoring the surface difficulties, are able to concentrate the mind on the essential Gospel contained in the various books of the Bible.

Volumes in the series include:

THE EPISTLE TO THE HEBREWS

Introduction and Commentary

by

WILLIAM NEIL
M.A., B.D., Ph.D.
Warden of Hugh Stewart Hall
University of Nottingham

SCM PRESS LTD
56 BLOOMSBURY STREET LONDON WC1

First published 1955
Second Impression 1959

Printed in Great Britain by
Northumberland Press Limited
Gateshead on Tyne

CONTENTS

5

*Chapter
and Verse*

PREFACE

I have written this commentary in a spirit of penitence. Hebrews was never a book which appealed to me very much as a student or even as a teacher of Biblical Studies. For obvious reasons it is not a part of the Bible that normally attracts our attention. Its general tone at first sight seems to be more remote from present day concerns than almost any other book in the New Testament.

Yet, as I have indicated in the Introduction, once the key is provided there is not only a treasure house of insights into Christian faith but also a specific relevance to twentieth century Church life and thought which is startling. For me the key was supplied by Professor William Manson's Baird Lecture for 1949, to which I owe a deep debt of gratitude. In writing this little commentary I have consulted all the standard works in English and German, but the particular angle from which Professor Manson has approached the epistle seems to me to shed new light on all the work that has previously been done on Hebrews.

I am further indebted to him in that he has kindly read this book in typescript and made many useful comments. My warm thanks are also due to my former colleague the Rev. Robert Davidson, M.A., B.D., of the Department of Biblical Studies in the University of Aberdeen, for his most helpful criticisms and for checking the biblical references.

W.N.

University of Nottingham
November 1954

BIBLIOGRAPHY

The following books in English and on the English text of the Epistle to the Hebrews will be found helpful:

WILLIAM MANSON, *The Epistle to the Hebrews* (Hodder & Stoughton).

F. D. V. NARBOROUGH, *Hebrews: Introduction and Commentary* (Clarendon Bible, O.U.P.).

A. S. PEAKE, *Hebrews* (Century Bible, T. C. and E. C. Jack).

T. H. ROBINSON, *Hebrews* (Moffatt New Testament Commentary Series, Hodder & Stoughton).

INTRODUCTION

THE EPISTLE TO THE HEBREWS

Generally speaking, if we want to do some Bible study with the help of a commentary we skip the Introduction and get down to business. The commentator, we feel, has probably a duty to his conscience to include a number of essays on the historical background, the identity of author and readers, the date of writing and the leading ideas of the particular book. None of all this, however, seems to matter very much when we are looking for what the Bible has to say to us to-day. It is rather like reading one of the Waverley Novels, where most of us promise ourselves to wade through Scott's Introduction some other time, but meanwhile we turn to the story.

In the case of the letter to the Hebrews, however, short cuts of this kind are barred. We cannot hope to understand its message for the twentieth century—assuming that it has one—until we have answered one or two prior questions of the kind we usually try to avoid. If we begin by cheerfully ignoring them we shall soon find ourselves floundering in what seems to be a morass of detail culled from the drearier stretches of the Pentateuch, including the furnishings of the Temple at Jerusalem, allusions to obscure patriarchs, and an ultra-Old Testament atmosphere which strikes us as more remote from the Gospel than almost anything else in the New Testament. Even when in the midst of this extremely Jewish setting we come upon some of the most breath-taking insights into the significance of Jesus, we are left with an overall impression that for the most part the

13

world which this letter reflects is not our world, and that its concerns are not our concerns. We may feel that while we doubtless share with the first readers of this letter one Lord, one Faith and one Baptism, we have little else in common with them and that other New Testament letters like Romans, Corinthians, and Philippians have much more to say to us to-day.

Nothing could be farther from the truth. We shall find that when we come to grips with the situation in which the first readers of this letter found themselves, it has remarkable points of contact with our own situation to-day. The factors which made it necessary for the Author of Hebrews to write this letter to them are operative in striking fashion again in the twentieth century. Danger from outside the Church and disillusionment within it were their lot as they are ours. The temptation to cling to the well-worn paths of traditional churchmanship and to shrink from the full implications of Christian discipleship is ours as well as theirs. We, like them, need to be reminded of the cost of obedience and the need of courage, but at the same time to be reassured as to the eternal validity of our Christian belief and the reality of our Christian hope.

WHO WROTE IT?

The official title in our English Bible is 'the Epistle of Paul the Apostle to the Hebrews'. This title is of course not original, and there is no indication as to the author within the letter itself. It seems to have been gradually attributed to St. Paul more for lack of a better known author than for any other reason. Our first impression is, however, that if this is a letter it is a very odd one. There is no customary opening greeting as in the normal Pauline letter and except for the last verse or two there are no personal references at all. It looks much more like a sermon which was intended to be read to some congregation,

and indeed the author himself calls it A WORD OF EXHORTA-
TION (13.22).

Our second impression is that it is very unlike any of the
other letters which we know to have been written by St.
Paul. Paul does not seem to have been particularly interested in all the elaborate technicalities of Jewish Temple
ritual. He is much more interested in Jewish moral law.
On the other hand he is probably best described as a man
'in Christ' on the grounds that a mystical faith-union with
the Risen Christ was for him the very essence of the
Christian life. But when we look at this letter we find that
its author is vastly concerned with what went on in the
Temple at Jerusalem, or in the Old Testament description
of it, which comes to the same thing, and that he never even
mentions faith-union with Christ.

Very early in the history of the Church, therefore, the
question was raised as to whether this was in fact one of
Paul's letters at all, and as far back as the third century
Origen made the classic comment 'Who wrote the Epistle
God only knows for certain'. In view of the many obvious
differences between Paul's style, language and interests and
those of the writer of Hebrews, the letter was not universally
acknowledged by the Church until late in the fourth century
on the ground that its authorship was so dubious. Various
guesses have been made as to who the author may have
been. The names of Barnabas, Luke, Silvanus, Philip,
Priscilla and Clement have all been canvassed. None of
these is as likely as Luther's candidate Apollos, the eloquent
Jewish-Christian preacher from Alexandria (Acts 18.24f.).
The oratorical style of the letter, the frequent Old Testament
quotations and the use made of them, combined with certain
distinctively Alexandrian features, would support Luther's
suggestion, which is, however, as much guess-work as the
others. In the commentary the writer will be referred to
simply as the Author.

Nowadays we are less inclined to worry about a question

of this kind. Most Old Testament books are of unknown authorship, and the fact that some New Testament books, which were thought at one time to be written by an apostle, turn out to be likewise anonymous, makes us rather realize how much richer the early Church was in theologians than we imagined.

WHERE TO, WHERE FROM, AND WHEN?

WHERE TO?

The letter is addressed to 'the Hebrews', which in Christian circles in New Testament times meant the more conservative Jewish Christians of Palestinian origin as opposed to the more liberal Greek-speaking Jewish Christians from overseas (Acts 6.1). The title was probably given to the epistle because it appeared to be directed to people who shared the narrower Palestinian point of view whether they lived there or not. It seems, however, that it was not meant for Jewish Christians of this type in general, but for a particular group of them (e.g. 5.11-12; 6.10-11; 13.19). Where this group may have been is again disputed. Jerusalem, Caesarea, Ephesus, Antioch, have all been suggested. The likeliest place is, however, Rome. The epistle was known and quoted in Rome earlier than anywhere else (by Clement of Rome in his letter to the Corinthians in A.D. 95) and the greeting in 13.24: THEY OF ITALY SALUTE YOU most probably implies that Christians from Italy, now living overseas beside the Author, wished to be remembered to the recipients.

WHERE FROM?

Again we can do no more than conjecture, but the evidence points to Alexandria. This had been already in Old Testament times the chief centre of Jewish life outside Palestine. Jewish immigrants had established there the Jewish way of life with Sabbath, Law and Synagogue within their own community, and in the process had attracted many pagan sympathisers, who felt that here were moral strength and social stability in a rapidly decaying Empire. For their own benefit, since they could no longer read Hebrew, these Alexandrian Jews used a Greek translation of the Old Testament. This version, called the Septuagint, proved from the third century B.C. onwards a most potent proselytising factor, since it opened the door to pagan interest and understanding. Many Jews went further and tried to show the connection between the thought of the Old Testament and Greek philosophy. Notably Philo, a first century A.D. Jew of Alexandria, sought to establish a bond between Plato and the Jewish faith. More than any other New Testament book Hebrews reflects these conditions. It is of a Jewish Christian character, but lacks the local knowledge that a Palestinian background would ensure. The Author quotes from the Greek version of the Old Testament, which he interprets allegorically in the Alexandrian fashion, and he makes copious use of the Platonic contrast between shadow and reality.

WHEN?

The date of composition can hardly be later than 95, since Clement of Rome makes allusion to this epistle in his letter to the Corinthians. Nor can it be earlier than St. Paul's letters, since there are traces of Pauline influence in the writing. A date therefore between A.D. 60-90 would seem to be appropriate. Some help may be given by the reference to the recipients in 2.3, suggesting that they were the second generation of Christians, and by the fact that the destruction of the Temple at Jerusalem in A.D. 70 is not mentioned, although it would have clinched the Author's argument that the death of Christ had now made the sacrificial ritual of the Temple otiose. The most we can say is that if the previous outbreak of persecution referred to in 10.32-34 refers to the expulsion of the Jews and Christians from

B

Rome by Claudius in A.D. 49 (Acts 18.2), then the current persecution alluded to in 12.4 would most probably be that of Nero, which came to a head in A.D. 64, after the Great Fire of Rome. The letter would then most likely date from the first shadows of Nero's persecution, perhaps soon after A.D. 60.

WHY WAS IT WRITTEN?

Although on the surface this Epistle to the Hebrews might seem to be concerned largely with Jewish priests and Jewish ritual, it is in fact a profoundly Christian appeal to trust in God come what may. It is written to people who are passing through a critical period in their Christian life. Part of the trouble is State interference. The conflict between Church and State which resulted in widespread persecution and martyrdom, until the Roman Empire became officially Christian under Constantine in A.D. 313, showed signs of developing almost from the beginning of the Church's history. The Roman government tolerated any religion that did not seem to impinge on its political rights. Christians and Jews, however, took their religion more seriously than others, and showed their disapproval of the lax standards of paganism plainly enough to make themselves highly unpopular. There were many other contributory factors to the growth of opposition on the part of the State and the deterioration of relations between the Church and the Government. But even from the beginning it was never an easy thing to be a Christian and to avow it openly. It invited contempt, or ostracism, or active hostility, and, later, confiscation of property, imprisonment and death.

The evidence of the epistle points to this as one of the factors which made this WORD OF EXHORTATION necessary. It is to encourage men and women who were holding fast to their faith against all opposition, and to warn those who were in danger of compromising. The Author meets this problem by holding up the example of Jesus, who had to suffer as they were suffering, but who showed how suffering should be borne, and who by his victory over death had ensured a like victory for his people. To deny him now would be to crucify him afresh (6.6).

Until very recently it appeared that a good case could be made out for believing that the readers of the letter were either Jewish Christians, who were in danger of lapsing into their former Jewish faith under threat of persecution, or ex-pagans who in similar circumstances found the attractions of their former beliefs stronger than their Christian convictions. Professor William Manson has, however, within the past few years,[1] put forward a view which seems to fit the evidence better than any theory previously advanced, and in addition brings the message of Hebrews into the closest association with twentieth century movements within the Church.

It is clear from the New Testament generally, that there was bitter opposition from the side of the Jews to the faith which claimed to have superseded Judaism. It is also clear, however, that within the young Christian Church itself there was considerable tension between those who cherished the legacy of Israel, and wished to embody it in its entirety in the Church, and those who, while recognizing their debt to Israel, nevertheless saw the future growth of the Church in a wider setting. St. Paul himself was, of course, the man who made it finally possible for Jews and Gentiles to enter the Christian Church on completely equal terms, but we must not neglect in this connection the pioneering work of Stephen. If we examine carefully the narrative of Acts 6 and 7 it would seem that this able Jew saw clearly that Jesus was more than a Jewish Messiah, and that the ' Way ', as Christianity was then called, was to be more than a sect of the Jewish Church.

His speech in Acts 7 is a call to his more conservative

[1] *The Epistle to the Hebrews*, 1951.

countrymen to recognize the world-mission of Jewry, no longer as the Old Israel but as part of the New Israel, the Christian Church. His appeal was to men who had distorted the mission of Israel into racial privilege and religious exclusiveness. The stones that killed him were their response to his challenge. His dying vision of Jesus as Son of Man (7.56), the ruler of the New Community drawn from all nations, as foreseen in Daniel 7.13, pinpoints his appreciation of the ecumenical nature of the Church. Manson's view is that the Author of Hebrews was writing to a group of Christian Jews, perhaps a house-congregation within the mixed Christian community of Rome, who shared the reluctance of Stephen's audience to face the world-mission of the New Israel. They were men to whom the traditions and worship of the Old Testament faith were so dear that they sought to retain the whole gamut of Judaism, together with its exclusiveness, as essential to the health of Christianity. To them the Author of our epistle utters a clarion call to face the realities of their Christian vocation in relation to the world at large. The New Age has dawned, the New Exodus has begun, the New Covenant has been established. Israel born anew must treasure the essence of its spiritual heritage, but its summons is now to proclaim it to the world. God has come among men through his Messiah and recalled his people to their proper obedience. The Old Testament faith is not abrogated but perfected. Second Isaiah's insight into the true role of Israel as a missionary people to bring the world to the knowledge of God must now be restated in terms of the Christian *ecclesia*.

Thus the essential purpose of the letter is a summons to stake everything on the intention of God to win the world back to himself through the activity and witness of the Church. It is a challenge to faith that, despite all appearance to the contrary, it is God's will that the whole world and not just one people should be won for Christ. This is no time, says the Author, for nostalgic yearnings over traditional modes of worship and familiar and conventional ways of approaching God, but a time for adventure, for taking courage in both hands and going out into the hazardous unknown future as did Abraham, Moses and the great men of Israel, trusting in the unseen God. The call is to leave the shelter and security of well-worn paths and to go forth outside the camp of Israel (13.13) to Jesus who beckons men to him, inviting them to share the hardships and penalties of Christian witness, as those who know that in this world they have no permanent resting place, but look forward to the end of their crusading in the presence of God.

WHAT THE LETTER IS ABOUT

If this epistle is indeed correctly seen as a contribution to Christian propaganda for the world-mission of the Church, it can be no longer true to regard it primarily as an attempt to restate the gospel in terms of Greek philosophy as has sometimes been maintained. It is the case, of course, that Christianity began in a totally Jewish setting. Jesus and the apostles were Palestinians, who talked and thought like first century Jews. The form in which the gospel was first proclaimed was one which was suited to people who had been brought up in the narrow confines of a small oriental country, whose minds had been conditioned by the views of God, man and the universe which were held by the writers of the Old Testament. Accordingly when the Church began to move out of this Palestinian environment and tried to make its message intelligible to non-Jews, it had to restate and reinterpret the gospel in language that would be understood by the ordinary citizens of the Graeco-Roman world.

These people had been brought up in a civilization far different from that of Palestine. Although the inhabited world was dominated by the Roman Empire and was under the authority of the Caesars, it was in effect a world whose cities, habits, language and customs derived from Greece. The empire of Alexander the Great had become Roman in name and in political power, but its intellectual and cultural life was still modelled on the Greek pattern.

St. John and St. Paul, as can easily be seen by comparing their language with that of the Synoptic Gospels, were both trying to reinterpret the original Palestinian gospel in a way that would be meaningful to their audiences in the Graeco-Roman world. This is no less true of the Author of our epistle, despite the fact that superficially it appears to have a thoroughly Jewish flavour. For when he emphasizes and re-emphasizes the claim that the difference between Judaism and Christianity is that between shadow and reality, he is using a concept which is familiar to all readers of Plato's *Republic*, and which would be particularly arresting to Jews living outside of Palestine. Not only had they absorbed some of the *Weltanschauung* of their Hellenistic neighbours, but in particular their own countryman Philo had already shown how Plato and the Law and Prophets of Israel could be reconciled.

Our Author, however, is not engaged in any such studied attempt to square the Gospel with Alexandrian philosophy. His purpose as we have seen lies in a different direction. He does, however, very properly make use of a popular and recognized feature of Greek thought to press his point home.

This Platonic contention that everything on earth has its ideal counterpart in heaven is indeed the major motif of the Author's argument. What we see here is imperfect and finite, the mere shadow of the perfect heavenly reality. So, says the epistle, is the relationship between Jewish practice and the Christian Gospel. What the religion of the Temple at Jerusalem was trying to do by means of animal sacrifice was to bridge the gulf between God and man, to restore the proper relationship which was perpetually broken by man's sinful acts and evil disposition. Priesthood, altar, and offerings: the elaborate ritual of the Day of Atonement, when the High Priest made intercession on behalf of the whole people: the strict observance of levitical succession: the punctilious ordering of ceremonial: were all designed to serve the one end, namely to enable men to live at peace with God. And this, says the Author, is precisely what Judaism could not do because it was earthbound. The best of man's activity is imperfect and fallible. Priests, sacrifices and ritual alike are but the shadowy reflection of reality. They could not accomplish what they set out to do. Only the heavenly reality could do that.

Over against them, and superseding them, stands Jesus Christ, God's own Son, the ideal Priest, who made the ideal Sacrifice, on the ideal Altar. By his offering of himself as the perfect Sacrifice once and for all Christ bridged the gulf between God and man, making man at one with God, creating a new relationship into which by faith in him all men could now enter. With the coming of Christ, reality had entered this shadowy world. Heaven came down to earth in Jesus in order that earthbound men might be raised to heaven.

ITS MESSAGE FOR TO-DAY

Much of the reasoning of this epistle is unfamiliar and irrelevant to-day. We are not first century Jews, and although we recognize our debt to the Old Testament it is a restricted allegiance. If the Old Testament faith and practice had been adequate there would have been no need for Christ and his Gospel. The appurtenances of the Temple at Jerusalem, the regulations of its priesthood and sacrifices have for Christians no more than antiquarian interest. Like-wise, far-fetched Old Testament exegesis and obscure Old Testament characters, like Melchizedek, have little or no interest for us to-day.

On the other hand, when we penetrate beneath the surface

of the letter, we find much that is supremely relevant to this and every other age. Here is a writer who stresses on the one hand the real humanity of Jesus, TEMPTED LIKE AS WE ARE YET WITHOUT SIN (4.15), and, on the other, his eternal and unchanging divinity, THE SAME YESTERDAY AND TO-DAY AND FOR EVER (13.8). He insists that the basic need of man is to be at one with God, and that the only way to that right relationship is through Christ, through whom we pass from the world of shadows into the world of reality. The Author reminds us that our best service is tainted with imperfection, and that our only hope of drawing near to God is by trusting him whose perfect obedience even to the point of death was the only perfect service and the perfect offering once made for all mankind. Through faith in that perfect offering made by Christ we can here and now experience the fellowship of the eternal God. By such a faith Christian men and women can overcome every trial that besets them (11.32-12.2).

Within our own day a revived interest in typology, which means the recognition in the Old Testament of fore-shadowings or patterns of New Testament events, makes it easier for us to appreciate the thought of the writer. We have learned that the proper attitude to the Old Testament is neither a slavish literalist approach, whereby we exalt its theology to the level of the New Testament and see in its writers infallible guides to science as well as to past, present and future history, nor a dismissal of its contents as a modicum of truth embedded in a mass of legend and superstition, but a recognition that what God was saying to Israel and doing in Israel was directly pointing to what he said and did in Christ and what he says and does to-day.

The twin pattern of Judgement and Mercy foreshadowed in the Old Testament is the eternal mode of God's dealing with men. Exodus, Covenant, Law, Sacrifice and Priesthood, which feature largely in this epistle, are meaningful facts, having their fulfilment in Christ. The faith of the patriarchs and the hopes of prophet and psalmist can be seen now likewise to have found their reality in him. The Author, with his rich store of Old Testament background, and despite some exegetical eccentricities, which were, however, valid arguments in his day, adds much to our understanding of how Old Testament and New Testament can be seen to form one continuous revelation.

Likewise the Author's summons to his readers to think ecumenically, in terms of the world mission of the Church, and to cling less tenaciously to familiar forms of worship as if they constituted the essence of their faith, is also timely for our day. We might ask ourselves whether our particular views of ministry and sacraments, of form and order, are any more essential to the health of the whole Body of Christ than were the equally cherished and historically defensible practices to which the readers of this letter were apparently attached. In view of the forces arrayed against the Church to-day, a neo-paganism more deadly than that of the first century, we may well heed the Author's warning against busying ourselves with theological hair-splitting over the rudiments of our faith (6.1), against fostering separatist and exclusive tendencies (13.24), and take to heart his call for deeds, not words. We may well ask ourselves whether traditions that we ourselves hold dear are bulking more largely in our minds than the primary task of carrying the Christian warfare for the souls of men right to the frontiers, and with a united front battling to win the whole world on every level of its life for Jesus Christ.

So also at a period of history when it is being borne in upon us more and more that the visible world is perishable and impermanent, that progress is an illusion, that change and decay are of the very essence of being, that new evils wax more easily than old ones wane, that hazard and insecurity are of the warp and woof of life, and that on no one day can we tell what the next will bring forth, the Author's reminder is apt that here we are but pilgrims on a journey whose end is not in sight nor in this world. We are

called to embark upon it in the spirit of Abraham, who was
content to strike no permanent roots on earth because his
goal was the City whose builder and maker is God. It is
good for us to be reminded that twentieth century question
marks are more akin to the greatest period of the Church's
faith and witness than nineteenth century certainties, and
to be forced, as were the early Christians, to recognize that
the only security for those who live in this world is to be
anchored to the world beyond. It is there that the mission
of the Church of which we are part finds its end in the New
Jerusalem of which the Author paints so striking a picture
(12.22-24).

Hebrews reminds us too that while St. Paul found life ' in
Christ' to be the ultimate heart of what Christianity meant
for him, and made Christ-mysticism the norm of Christian
experience, nevertheless he did not neglect the complemen-
tary summons to Christian discipleship, which is also part
of the original gospel. If we cannot aspire to St. Paul's sense
of self-identification with the Risen Christ, we may be better
able, with the Author, to run the race that is set before us,
looking unto Jesus, the Pioneer and Perfecter of our Faith
(12.1-2).

COMMENTARY

I

THE SIGNIFICANCE OF JESUS
1.1-3

The view of the Author, like that of all the other biblical writers, is that what we know about God, man and the universe is just what God has chosen to disclose and no more. In other words, our knowledge of God is not merely the result of our quest for the truth, but of God's intention that the truth should be known. While that knowledge comes partly through science, philosophy, literature, art, music and the world around us, God has chosen in a special way to communicate the truth about his nature and purpose to a particular community in a particular period of history, and so through them to the rest of the world.

We have therefore to see these first few verses in their proper perspective which is God's scheme of salvation as recorded in the Bible as a whole. God created men and women to live in perfect harmony with himself and with each other. We were meant to be sons and daughters of God (Gen. 1-2). By our self-will, pride, lust, greed and folly we have failed to fulfil his purpose and made havoc of our own lives and the life of the world (Gen. 3-11). The Bible from Genesis 12 onwards is the story of what God has done and is doing to recreate us into the sons and daughters we were meant to be. For the writer to the Hebrews, as for all other biblical writers, God's purpose is that men should be brought back into the proper relationship with himself and with their fellow men. Reconciliation is in a sense the key-word of Old and New Testaments.

Here the writer places right at the forefront of his letter a magnificent summary of the redemptive acts of God which the Bible describes. Having made himself and his intention partially known to and through Israel, the community which he selected for this purpose, he has now finally not only disclosed all that men need to know to be at one with God but has also done what needed to be done to establish that right relationship by means of Jesus Christ. The mind of God, the purpose that underlies the universe, the nature of ultimate reality, has now been expressed in terms of human personality. The entrance of Christ on to the stage of history is its most decisive hour, the culmination of revelation, the key to all knowledge of God. It is the most significant moment since Creation.

1. God having spoken in the prophets

This does not mean that the Old Testament prophets were merely mechanical mouthpieces. When a prophet said 'Thus saith the Lord' he put into words convictions which came to him as he reflected on the life of his times in the light of his own faith and apprehension of the will of God.

by divers portions and in divers manners

We now understand better than our grandfathers did what is meant by these words. God only discloses such aspects of himself and his purpose as can be grasped by a particular person at a particular time. Amos was given an insight into the Justice of God. Hosea was enabled to see his Mercy, Isaiah learned of his Holiness. No single prophet, from Moses onwards, could know or declare the whole truth about God, but each in his own way was shown some part of the truth. Probably in these words (lit. 'in many parts and in many forms') the writer means to include not only the prophets but all the avenues by which God gave the revelation of himself to Israel and which together

make up the Old Testament. But all this was fragmentary.
The full revelation of God could only come through someone who was himself one with God.

2. has spoken in his son

Just as we are to understand God's 'speaking' in Old
Testament times in the widest sense, including the things
that he did, so, here, more is meant than the teaching of
Jesus. What is implied is the whole activity of Christ, in
disclosing the nature and purpose of God, from Incarnation
to Ascension. Part of the Old Testament revelation had
been the hope of the coming of one who would bring the
power and wisdom of God into ordinary life. To the early
Church it seemed that with one voice psalmists and prophets
spoke of this appearance of God's anointed representative,
Messiah, as the climax of history and the beginning of a
new era (Ps. 2.1-9; 89.19-27; 110.1-4; Isa. 2.2-4; 9.6-7;
11.1-10). The whole of the Old Testament appeared to
them to point forward to this event which they claimed had
now happened.

at the end of these days

The prophets, when they viewed the harassed and dis-
traught times in which they lived, and looked towards a day
when God would be everywhere acknowledged and show
his power by banishing evil from the world, tended to think
of this Golden Age as coming about without a major up-
heaval. As life grew more difficult for the Jews in the
centuries before the Christian era they gave up hope of any
such change taking place in the world as they knew it. So
corrupt and unjust a state of affairs could not be put right
without some dramatic *dénouement*. Thus arose the conviction that one day God would rise in his wrath and put
an end to the sorry thing that the world had become. His
Messiah would appear and after a cataclysmic end to the
existing world-order a new heaven and new earth would

take its place and Messiah would reign over God's faithful people while their oppressors would perish or suffer the torments of the damned.

The primary proclamation of the apostles after Pentecost was that this was what had begun to happen. Messiah had come. Jesus of Nazareth had been he. Though men in their wickedness had done to death God's Anointed, God had proved him to be Messiah by raising him from the dead. The Resurrection, the apostolic miracles, the outpouring of the Spirit at Pentecost were all signs that the end of the old order was fast approaching. Soon the world that men knew would reach its appointed terminus. Messiah would return and the Kingdom of God would come to stay.

This was the background to the thinking of the early Church including the New Testament writers. It is a thoroughly Jewish concept founded on a world view which was time-conditioned and which needs to be reinterpreted for our own day. But basically it is as valid and profound an insight in the twentieth century as in the first. It maintains that with the coming of Christ the old order ended and the New Order began. A new power, the power of God's spirit working through Christ's people, the Christian Church, is at work in the world. The Church lives in the expectation of the final triumph of its Master and in the conviction that in the fulness of God's time evil will be destroyed and God's will be done. History will have an end and beyond that end lies the consummation of God's purpose, the perfect fellowship of God's children with himself and with one another through Christ. Meanwhile, Christ's people enjoy the foretaste of that perfect end through their communion with God in the society of the Church on earth.

In the earliest days of the Church, however, so intense was the sense that the New Order had begun that men could not believe that the final victory of God would be long delayed. Hence the atmosphere of expectancy which pervades the New Testament writings. The fact that when the end did not come the faith of the Church was not shattered is the best indication that the basic conviction was not the time factor, but the sense of living already in a new dimension. The Author of Hebrews does not share the cruder form of apocalyptic hope, as for example we find it in the Book of Revelation. Such a phrase as 'the end of these days' therefore, while it reflects the universal sense of the impending end of the world as men knew it, is basically an expression of the conviction that the decisive hour in history had now struck, that God had in a signal way entered the ordinary life of men. For Christian people that meant that they more than the rest of mankind were conscious of standing under the Judgement of God and that they must so live that if it pleased God to erase the old order finally at any moment they would be prepared to meet him face to face. This is equally cogent for the Church to-day.

Son

It is worth noting that the Greek does not say 'in his Son' but 'in a son' (i.e. in one who is Son), as if not only to distinguish between any kind of revelation that had gone before and that given through Christ, but also to stress the unique place of Christ in the universe. What the writer means by 'son' he now goes on to say, and it should be observed that the same things are said in different words throughout the New Testament. This was what the early Church as a whole thought about Jesus.

whom he appointed heir of all things

Here Jesus is identified with the Old Testament Messiah. God's blessing was promised to Israel, his people, who are sometimes referred to as his son (e.g. Hos. 11.1). On occasion the King of Israel, as representative of his people, is also so described (e.g. II Sam. 7.14). But above all the Messianic King of psalm and prophecy is looked on as God's

heir, the inheritor of the promises of God to his people
(e.g. Ps. 2.1-9; Isa. 11.1-10). Jesus spoke of himself as the
Heir in the parable of the vineyard (Mark 12.1-10), implying
his unique relationship to God and his authority over the
vineyard, which is, of course, Israel. Here the meaning is
that Jesus inherits, on behalf of the New Israel, the assurance
of God's presence, power and loving-kindness which were
promised to the Old Israel.

through whom also he made the worlds

This identifies Jesus with the creative power of God. In
the Old Testament, Creation is attributed to the Word of
God (Gen. 1.3: AND GOD SAID, LET THERE BE LIGHT) or to
the Wisdom of God (Prov. 8). In the intertestamental period
(e.g. Wisdom of Solomon 7.21f.) the Word or Wisdom of
God was thought of almost as a personal emanation of God.
As such it could easily be related, as was done for example
by Philo, to the Logos of Greek philosophy, which was
regarded as the immanent Reason which created and
directed the universe.

The attribution of pre-existence to Jesus springs primarily
from his own self-consciousness and his identification of
himself with the Father. If Jesus was what he claimed to
be, and had the power that only God could have to heal,
forgive and change men's lives, it followed that he must have
been present eternally with God. One aspect of the Wisdom-
Logos idea was that it made possible communication between God and man, and this was precisely the role that
the Christian missionaries credited to Jesus. Their interest
in the Wisdom-Logos idea was thus not primarily philo-
sophical but theological and missionary. The conviction of
the early Church was that the ultimate purpose of God had
now been expressed in Christ. In using terminology like
'Logos' or 'Word' (e.g. John 1.1-4, 14), or in other ways
identifying Jesus with the creative and sustaining power
behind the universe (e.g. here and also Col. 1.14-17), the

New Testament writers were trying to translate the Messiah and all that he meant for those brought up in the Jewish tradition into language and concepts which were more familiar to the Graeco-Roman world.

3. the effulgence of his glory

Jesus was the visible and comprehensible expression of the light and power and holiness of God which are beyond man's understanding.

the very image of his substance

This is a metaphor from a seal. The wax bears the exact reproduction of the stamp. Jesus' character is the express image of God's own.

upholding all things by the word of his power

The mysterious cosmos which terrifies us by its immensity is not a cold impersonal series of galaxies stretching out to infinity, but a universe directed and controlled by one whom Jesus has revealed as Love.

when he had made purification of sins

This is the first mention of that aspect of our Lord's work which is to form the main content of the epistle.

sat down on the right hand of the majesty on high

This symbolic phrase (cf. Ps. 110.1: Mark 16.19) suggests the royal authority of one who sits while subjects stand or kneel, the attitude of one whose chief task is now accomplished, and the status of one whose relationship to God is unique. It is no weakness of a phrase of this sort that it lays itself open to the charge of anthropomorphism. When we talk about God our language is bound to be limited by our human understanding, and our inability to express divine truth in anything other than human terms. Jesus himself was boldly anthropomorphic in all his teaching about God. When he calls himself God's Son it is a human symbol, but

C

is there any better simple way of describing the uniqueness
of Jesus' relationship to God?

JESUS IN THE OLD TESTAMENT
1.4-14

While at first sight these verses appear to be a collection
of Old Testament quotations indicating the superiority of
Christ over angels, they are rather to be seen as an illuminating illustration of how the Old Testament derived new meaning for the Church as the early Christians saw in it a
treasure-house of insight into the person of Christ. The
quotations come from a variety of Old Testament sources,
but they are all regarded as of Messianic significance.
Whether they are originally used of God himself (as Ps.
102.25-27 in v. 10) or of historical or ideal kings of Israel
(as Ps. 110.1 in v. 13) they are now related directly to Christ.
He is regarded either as synonymous with God, to be
equated with God, or he is regarded as the fulfilment of all
that is said in the Old Testament about God's Anointed,
whether people, kings, or Messiah of Israel. He is God's
Son, his chosen one, who sums up in himself all partial and
shadowy representations of Messiah, be they historical
figures or the subject of the hopes and prayers of prophet
and psalmist. In thus regarding Christ as not only pre-
existent but present throughout all Israel's history the
Author of Hebrews agrees again with St. John and St. Paul
(e.g. John 1.5: I Cor. 10.4).

It should be noted that throughout the epistle the Author
is quoting from the Greek version of the Old Testament.
Our English A.V. and R.V. are translations of the original
Hebrew. Where there are discrepancies between Old Testament quotations in the epistle and the Old Testament itself,
the reason is the variation, which is not great, but on
occasion confusing, between the Hebrew original and the
Greek translation.

THE PROBLEM OF THE ANGELS

The occasion of this catena of Old Testament quotations is the assertion in v. 4 that the attributes of Christ which have been described in vv. 1-3 place him in a vastly more exalted position than the angels. Angels appear infrequently in the Old Testament. When they do so they are primarily messengers of God, sometimes in human guise (e.g. Gen. 18-19). In general, however, throughout most of the Old Testament, God is considered to be close enough to men to speak directly to them or by the mouth of psalmist or prophet.

From the time of the Babylonian exile, however, partly as a result of an increasing sense of the holiness of God and his remoteness from human evil, and partly through contact with the mythology of other religious systems, notably that of Persia, there arose the view that between God and man there existed a hierarchy of intermediate beings, part of whose business it was to bring messages to men from God and carry their prayers to him. In the intertestamental period, this belief grew and intensified until it reached the point reflected in the folk-tales of the Apocrypha where guardian angels, archangels, and myriads of ordinary angels were held responsible for all good things that happened on earth, just as their equivalents in the demon world were reckoned to be the instruments of all evil. This belief in angels and demons is of course part of the texture of the gospel narratives.

ANGEL WORSHIP

In asserting the supremacy of Christ over all such angelic beings the Author may simply be adding a further item to the series of attributes in vv. 1-3. Those commentators who see the main point of the letter to be an attack on the same type of incipient heresy as in Colossians find no difficulty in explaining the Author's preoccupation with this problem.

Exotic beliefs of various sorts, including angel-worship, the product of the amalgam of western and oriental religious thought which Hellenistic civilization encouraged, threatened to corrupt the apostolic faith. That Christ had opened the way to God without the need of intercession by intermediary angelic powers was a fundamental tenet of the missionaries. Such may indeed have been the point in the Author's mind.

GIVERS OF THE LAW

It is equally possible however, and more consonant with other evidence in the epistle (e.g. 2.5), that the introduction of angels here is directly concerned with the traditionalism of the recipients. If they were indeed too eager to retain within the Christian Church the practices commended in Jewish Law, they would regard these words as directed sharply to themselves. For it was accepted at this stage of Jewish belief that while Moses had been responsible for communicating the Law to Israel, Moses himself had received it not directly from God but from angels (Acts 7.51-53; Gal. 3.19). In insisting on the primacy of Christ, therefore, the Author is skilfully striking his first blow to undermine the authority of the Law in the minds of his readers. Only by proving from scripture itself that Christ was superior to the guardians of the Law could the Author proceed to assert its inadequacy and its supersession by a higher authority.

II

THE DANGER OF DRIFTING
2.1-5

Having shown by his series of Old Testament texts that the place of the Son in God's scheme of things is far superior to that of angels, the Author now goes on to draw the conclusion. The word spoken through angels, namely the Law, must be inferior to the word spoken through the Lord, namely the Gospel. He strikes a note of grave warning on the danger of drifting away from the truth as revealed in Christ (v. 1). Even the Law exacted heavy penalities for disregarding its provisions. How much more serious would it be to fail to take advantage of the new life offered by Christ (vv. 2-3).

As we have seen, the question of what may be meant by 'drifting' may be answered in various ways. No specific danger is mentioned, but the language suggests that the readers were failing to realize the full implications of the Gospel rather than that they were guilty of any flagrant lapses into paganism like the Corinthians or Gnostic errors like the Colossians. They are encouraged to anchor themselves to the Gospel in all its fulness. This was no angelic message but the Word of God himself. It was declared first through Christ, and here as in 1.2 we are to think not only of the teaching of Jesus, but the whole saving work of Christ, his Life, Death, and Resurrection (v. 3). Its final validity and divine power were further attested by those who had been witnesses of the Gospel events in Galilee and Jerusalem, and who had proclaimed them in the early stages of the mission. They had told also of the marvellous acts that had accompanied the proclamation of the Gospel: the healing of men's

minds and bodies, the sense of liberation for Jew and
Gentile, the new quality of life when the power of the Spirit
had come upon them at Pentecost (v. 4). This was no dead
tradition but a living, energizing, forward-looking faith. It
was the coming of the power of God into human life, the
breaking into time and space of the eternal order. And
the Lord of that eternal order is no mere angelic being but
Jesus Christ. Such is the world in which Christians live, not
in the world that men knew before Christ came (v. 5).

3. confirmed unto us by them that heard

Apart from any other evidence this phrase would dispose
of the possibility that Hebrews was written by St. Paul. He
always claimed that he preached the Gospel by the direct
authority of Christ himself in virtue of his experience on
the Damascus road. Although he like other missionaries
inherited the theological framework of the Gospel (e.g. I Cor.
15.3f.), he did not rely on second-hand evidence either of the
reality of salvation or of the validity of his proclamation
of it.

4. the gifts of the Holy Ghost

Doubtless in the first days of the Christian mission the
ecstatic atmosphere of Pentecost, highly charged with
emotionalism, and productive of scenes comparable to
religious revivals in modern times, was regarded as the
surest proof that the Spirit of God had come among men as
foretold by the prophet Joel (2.28-32). At the same time,
however, the gifts of the Holy Ghost were more correctly
seen to be LOVE, JOY, PEACE, LONG-SUFFERING, KINDNESS,
GOODNESS, FAITHFULNESS, MEEKNESS, TEMPERANCE (Gal.
5.22-23). The changed lives of the first Christians, notably
St. Paul himself, were the best indication that supernatural
power was at work in the Church. St. Paul grapples with
this problem in I Cor. 12 and 14.

THE FULFILMENT OF MAN'S DESTINY
ASSURED THROUGH CHRIST
2.6-18

The Author is now leading up to his main theme, which is the death of Jesus and what it accomplished for the salvation of the world. His argument moves to this new aspect of Christology, now that he has established the supremacy of Christ over angels, and therefore of the Gospel over the Law. As a prelude to that he shows that what Jesus did in becoming man for the space of his earthly ministry was to stoop down to man's level in order to raise man up to God's. He quotes Ps. 8, which asserts that man is ranked only a little lower than the angels in God's ordering of the universe and that everything in it is under man's control.

9. crowned with glory and honour

Now, says the Author, this is obviously not the case. Man is not master of his fate. He is at the mercy of forces stronger than himself—the power of evil, senescence, death. On the other hand one Man as we can see *was* master of his fate. One Man defeated the power of sin, proved himself stronger than evil, and above all stronger than death. He alone is now CROWNED WITH GLORY AND HONOUR as the Psalmist put it. Therefore the Psalmist could not have been speaking about mankind in general, but about one Man, the Perfect Man, the Son of Man. He must have meant the Representative Man, man as God wanted man to be, not man as he is. (Notice the parallel with St. Paul's thought of Christ as the Second Man: Adam of Gen. 1 and 2 being Man as he is, while Christ is Man as he was intended to be (I Cor. 15.22f.)).

a little lower than the angels

Christ was able to fulfil this role, and on behalf of mankind to reach the status of GLORY AND HONOUR which God had purposed for it, because he was content to be for A LITTLE TIME LOWER THAN THE ANGELS and to endure the humiliation of man's lot including suffering and death. His present exaltation is the guarantee that man through him will yet attain to the destiny allotted to him by God, the status of which the Psalmist spoke. He became like us in order that we might become like him.

Since the main concern of the Author is with the High Priesthood of Jesus, he thinks primarily of the suffering and death of Christ as focusing the humiliation of his incarnate life. Although he would of course have regarded the whole of the earthly ministry of Jesus, his words and works, as the giving of himself for man, it is in the supreme sacrifice of Christ that he sees the accomplishment of man's salvation. Yet even in the act of self-offering throughout the whole incarnate life of our Lord, we see him already CROWNED WITH THE GLORY AND HONOUR that lie ahead. It was as much of a temptation then as now to think of 'glory and honour' in terms of success, and, in the case of God, in terms of omnipotence, rather than in terms of service and self-sacrifice. The example of Christ teaches us otherwise.

by the grace of God

Some of the early Christian writings quoting this verse have, instead of the Greek word for 'by the grace of', the word for 'apart from'. This might either refer to Jesus' sense of dereliction upon the Cross (Mark 15.34) or might mean that he died for everyone except God. More probably it is an example of how a scribe added the latter pious comment in the margin which in process of copying strayed into the text and came to replace the original. TASTE DEATH i.e. savour all the bitterness of death (cf. Jesus' own use of the metaphor of drinking the cup of death—Mark 10.38-39).

10. it became him

i.e. God. This is not a case of the Author saying what

was right or wrong for God to do. He means that it was in keeping with God's nature as everywhere revealed. God's GRACE (v. 9) or love for men, his sons, was so great that no price was too great to pay for their deliverance even if it meant that his own Son should become man and share all man's defeats and heartbreaks. GOD SO LOVED THE WORLD . . . (John 3.16). This is the only direct reference in Hebrews to the love of God as being the motive behind the Atonement.

the author of their salvation

A better word would be ' captain ' as in A.V. or ' pioneer '. The idea is that of Jesus opening up a new way and leading mankind to the destiny for which it was created. In order to bring his sons (not only Christian men but all men) to glory, i.e. the perfect relationship with himself and all that follows from that, God had to provide a Leader, who through sharing all the hardship and bitter experience of human life, the sorrows and temptations of ordinary men (' SUFFER-INGS '), would learn the sympathy and understanding that are essential for perfect Leadership. To readers who were themselves aware of the sufferings of persecution and the threat of martyrdom this point would seem specially relevant. They will be reminded later in the letter (12.5-11) that the path to ' GLORY AND HONOUR ' for them involves sharing the suffering which their Leader has already undergone and which he has shown them how to bear.

11. are all of one (father)

The universal Fatherhood of God and Brotherhood of Christ. Christ came to bring the *whole world* back to God.

14. the Devil

In the Old Testament the Devil, or Satan, appears but seldom. God was held to be responsible for sudden death and disaster as well as for all good things, on the ground

that when evil things happened it was considered to be justly
deserved punishment for sin. Satan features only in the later
stages of the Old Testament as causing evil by God's per-
mission (e.g. Job 1.6f.). Such a facile answer was however
felt to be inadequate and, partly through foreign influence
and partly through a deeper recognition of the problem,
there grew up in intertestamental times the conception of
the double order: the Kingdom of God and the Kingdom of
Satan. Under God the angels were responsible for the good
fortunes of men, under Satan the demons prompted all their
evil actions and were the cause of disease, insanity and
death. The Church of the New Testament inherited this
conception and accepted it. It was the framework in which
Jesus expressed his own mission. He had come as God's
Messiah to do battle with Satan, and he regarded his healing
of men's bodies and minds as signs that the power of God
was stronger than that of the Devil. He himself spoke of
casting out Satan, and of Satan's power tottering as a result
of Messiah's work and that of his followers (Mark 3.23f.;
Luke 10.18).

The conviction of the Church was that in principle Satan
had been defeated. Evil still flourished in the world and
would fight for the mastery until the final victory of Christ,
when he would reign supreme. The Church was summoned
to battle for Christ against the power of the Devil until the
end. But victory was assured since Christ had by his Resurrection wrested the power of death from Satan's hands. The
death of the body, epitomizing all the pain and suffering of
mankind, ruthless and relentless, irrational and hideous, and
more than death the terror of the unknown beyond, was the
thraldom from which Christ had delivered men. The empty
tomb was the symbol of Satan's downfall.

The Author's picture, therefore is one of Jesus as Leader
or Pioneer, entering the lists in flesh and blood, to do battle
with Satan on behalf of men and defeating him by his Resurrection. It is a picture which is suggested in other New

Testament writings (Col. 2.15: John 12.31) and one which would strike a chord in minds familiar with the mythology of the Graeco-Roman world where gods came down to earth to do battle for men. The fact that the Hellenistic mind would see it as a fairy-tale come true is no less reason for the early Church using familiar pagan concepts to communicate Christian truth, than for preaching the gospel to Jews in the equally mythological framework of Satan and his myrmidons. The basic truth for Jew and Gentile, and for us, is that through Christ death is swallowed up in victory.

That the Author is writing to Jews is borne out by the fact that he now goes on (v. 16) to say that what Christ came to succour was the SEED OF ABRAHAM (i.e. the Jewish nation), and proceeds to concentrate his argument on the High Priesthood of Jesus, which would mean little in those days for any other than ex-Jews. This reference to Christ's redemption of the Jews does not conflict with what has just been said of the universalism of the gospel. Christ came to rescue the whole of mankind from the corruption and frustration of the human situation. But first he came to the Jews. Then Jews and Gentiles together form the 'Israel of God' (Gal. 6.14-16).

17. it behoved him

Since Christ stood in the relationship of brotherhood to men he had to become like them in all respects, to share human experience to the full, including that of being tempted, suffering, and dying, in order that he might fulfil his High Priestly role of securing the forgiveness of men's sins. He could only intercede sympathetically for men if he knew himself the temptations to which they were subject. Without knowing himself the full range of human suffering and human temptation Jesus could not make man at one with God. The Author's viewpoint has been called Atonement by sympathy.

III

ONWARD! CHRISTIAN SOLDIERS
3.1-6

It will have become obvious by now that we are dealing with a writer who has an extraordinarily rich and subtle mind. Not for nothing has Hebrews been described as artistically the most impressive of the New Testament documents, and not for nothing did Luther guess the eloquent Apollos, skilled in the refinements of Alexandrian rhetoric, as the Author. So ingenious is the writer and so complex are the processes of his mind, ever suggesting fresh avenues of thought, then passing swiftly on, only to return again to develop the suggested idea at a later point, that we are in danger sometimes of losing the thread of his argument which runs like a golden cord through the maze of his quotations, allusions and cross-references.

Let us therefore get our perspective right. The main theme of the epistle is how men can get into the right relationship with God, a perennial problem which the Author, to suit the background and situation of his readers, discusses under the symbol of the High Priesthood of Jesus. This occupies the central part of the letter from 4.14 to 10.18. Within that major section there are naturally digressions, but by and large the point is made again and again that Christ and only Christ can bring us face to face with God and make us at one with him. Having seen that, we shall have little difficulty in following the Author in the practical conclusions which he draws for our Christian life in the last few chapters 10.19–13.25.

The first few chapters are a little more difficult. They are complicated by the introduction of the angels in chapters 1 and 2, and Moses and Joshua in chapters 3 and 4. Part of the difficulty arises from the fact that the Author is doing two things at the same time. He is in the first place demonstrating in language and thought-forms suitable for first century Jewish Christians that the Word spoken by God through Christ has now finally superseded the Word spoken by God through Moses and the angels.

In the second place, however, he is insisting that not only has the Gospel superseded the Law with all its ramifications, but also that for Christians the world that existed before the coming of Christ has now ceased to exist. They live in a New Order. They are called to take part in the New Exodus of the New Israel, in the march of the People of God to the Promised Land. Salvation has been proclaimed (2.3) and its end is not in this world (2.5). Christ the Pioneer is beckoning men to follow the path which he himself has trodden, a path which led through suffering to honour and glory (2.10). The passage which we are now to consider (3.1-4.13) contrasts the pilgrimage of the old Israel under Moses to the Land of God's Promise, with the crusade that Christians are called on to undertake in the world until they reach their Promised Land in the Presence of God.

1. holy brethren

In a moment the Author will be speaking of the Church as the household of God. The readers therefore as members of the family are brothers in Christ of the writer and of each other.

partakers of a heavenly calling

Through no merit of their own, but by the grace of God, they have been called, given the opportunity, of joining the forward march of God's People which ends in heaven.

the apostle and high priest of our confession

Jesus has already been referred to as HIGH PRIEST in 2.17.

This thought will be developed in the next chapter. Here he is also called APOSTLE, lit. one who is sent out, a messenger of God. The two words are related in that the High Priest on the Day of Atonement in the Jewish Temple was likewise called an Apostle. The obvious sense of CONFESSION here would be that the High Priesthood of Jesus was as much a part of the proclamation of the gospel as his Messiahship. There were many ways in which the significance of Jesus had to be communicated, depending on the nature and upbringing of the audience, whether Jewish or pagan. Since he was regarded as the fulfilment of all the thoughts and aspirations of mankind it would be unlikely that such a suggestive and important function as that of High Priest would be omitted. The fact that his High Priesthood is mentioned more than once in this epistle before the subject is taken up in detail would suggest that it was already a familiar designation. The early Church searched the scriptures for Messianic prophecies and the identification of Messiah with the PRIEST OF THE ORDER OF MELCHIZEDEK in Ps. 110 can hardly have been first discovered by the Author. It may well be, however, that its implications had never before been so fully drawn out as they are in this letter.

2. as also was Moses in all his house

The faithfulness or perfect obedience of Jesus, which has been mentioned already (2.17), is now compared to that of Moses. The allusion is to Num. 12.7. Moses' apparent high-handedness had aroused the displeasure of his brother Aaron and his sister Miriam. Yahweh however took both of them to task and announced that whereas he would communicate with the rank and file of Israel through the prophets, and even with them only through dream and vision, with Moses he would speak directly and he alone would see Yahweh face to face. The reason for this was that Moses alone was FAITHFUL IN ALL MINE HOUSE. By

'house' is meant of course Israel, the household of God.
In all matters affecting Old Israel therefore no one stood
higher in God's favour than Moses. He was God's means
of communication to men. Hence it was through Moses
that the Law, the rule of God for his people, was delivered
to Israel. But the Law had two aspects: the moral and
civil provisions that governed the conduct of men and the
life of society, and the cultic and ritual regulations that
governed their approach to God. This second aspect is the
one with which the Author is concerned. For Moses was
not only the founder of the Law on its moral and civil side
but on its priestly side as well. The priesthood of Israel
derived from Aaron, the brother of Moses (Ex. 28), but it
had been exercised before him and had been delegated to
him by Moses himself (Lev. 8). Thus on all counts no one
in all the history of Israel ranked higher than he.

Yet as the Author goes on to say (v. 3-6), Moses was at
best but a member of the household of God, and a servant
in it, whereas Christ is its founder; Christ is the heir (cf. 1.4)
who has now entered into his inheritance. Moses was the
servant who was in charge of the household until he came;
a custodian of God's revelation (the Law) until the greater
revelation (the Gospel) should be given. In this sense the
house is the same. It is still God's house. Moses and the
Law were caretakers in the days of Old Israel. Now that
the Son of the House has come into his own it is the house
of the New Israel. There is a parallel in St. Paul's figure
of the Law as a guardian until the child should be fully
grown (Gal. 3.23f.).

It is possible that the immediate occasion of this comparison between Moses and Christ may have been a com-
plaint on the part of the readers in Rome that the written
Law offered a security that had now disappeared. They
were asked to follow the guidance of the Spirit. The cast-
iron provisions of the Law, even if they could not be fulfilled,
made religious life more comfortable. If this is so the

Author's summons to boldness and to reliance on the Christian hope (v. 6) would serve to stress the essential difference in outlook between the Old and New Israel.

THE NEW EXODUS
3.7-19

The last note which the Author has sounded, the call to the New Israel to go forward boldly into the future with their eyes fixed on their heavenly goal, leads him on to a comparison between the Church's journey under the leadership of Christ and the Israelites' journey under Moses. Nothing is more certain than that the early Christians saw in the Exodus the same pattern as had become visible in their own experience. For the Old Testament writers the Exodus had been no mere 'going out'. It was a Deliverance, a signal act of God's mercy whereby a group of disinherited serfs were miraculously saved from slavery and ultimate extinction, and set on the road to freedom and shown the way to a new life. The Covenant at Sinai was the pledge of a new relationship to a God whom they had hitherto only dimly glimpsed.

It was no mere play on words that made Jesus call his own death an Exodus, a Deliverance (Luke 9.31), or speak at the Last Supper of a New Covenant (Mark 14.24). Nor was it fanciful allegorism that suggested to St. Paul that Christ was our Passover (I Cor. 5.7), and that Christian Baptism could be compared with the Crossing of the Red Sea (I Cor. 10.2). For essentially the conviction of the early Church was that by a greater and mightier act of God in history, a new Deliverance had been achieved, whereby Old Israel which had failed in its task had been transformed into a New Israel, and having entered into a New Covenant, a new relationship to God made possible through Christ, the Church had embarked upon a new journey through the wilderness of this world towards the Land of God's Promise.

So when the Author summons his readers to the active service of the living God (v. 12) he does so in the apostolic conviction that this is for the world the decisive hour. A new start has been offered, but also a final warning has been given. Failure now means failure for ever. Let the example of Israel's lack of faith spur them to new endeavour. The penalty in Israel's case was that they were kept out of the Promised Land for forty years. In the case of the New Israel the penalty would be to forfeit the Promised Land entirely, to miss eternal life in the presence of God.

The examples that the Author gives from the story of the old Exodus are illuminating. The first (v. 8f.) in the words of Ps. 95.7-11 describes the incident (Ex. 17.1-7) where Israel on its journey through the desert is afraid of perishing for lack of water and complains bitterly to Moses, sighing for the security of Egyptian servitude, where at least they had enough water to keep them alive. Hence the place was called Meribah or Provocation and Massah or Temptation, BECAUSE THEY TEMPTED (OR PROVOKED) THE LORD SAYING, IS THE LORD AMONG US, OR NOT?

The second example (v. 17) refers to the incident in Num. 13-14, where spies are sent out to view the Promised Land of Canaan. Back they come with tangible proof of a land flowing with milk and honey, but with the report that it was hedged in with enemies and populated by men of gigantic stature beside whom they felt like grasshoppers. Again Israel rebelled and sighed for the security of Egypt. Despite the assurances of their leaders and their appeals to trust in God's continuing protection, they refused to go forward. As a punishment they were condemned to remain in the wilderness for forty years, and were not allowed to enter their REST, i.e. to settle in Canaan (v. 11).

It is obvious that the basic sin in both cases was a refusal to put their trust in the God who had delivered them and to venture everything in that faith. It is equally obvious that the Author is not speaking of credal orthodoxy when

D

he urges his readers to TAKE HEED OF AN EVIL HEART OF UNBELIEF, but is summoning them to a like pilgrimage in vital dependence on the living God (v. 12). They are PARTAKERS, i.e. followers of Christ (v. 14), ranged behind their Leader who has pointed the way. For them (and us) it is the time of decision. The watchword is TODAY (v. 13), before today becomes yesterday. The opportunity will not come again.

17. forty years

It has been suggested that a special point in the repeated emphasis on forty years may be that when this letter was written there was a further parallel with the Exodus in that something like forty years had now elapsed since the New Exodus. This would put the date somewhere in the sixties of the first century A.D.

19. they were not able to enter in because of unbelief

No arbitrary act of God prevented them, but rather the inevitable result of their own sin. Notice how in this passage unbelief or lack of faith is equated with disobedience. It was their initial lack of faith that produced their disobedience. Conversely their disobedience was a proof that they lacked the right relationship to God, which is faith.

IV

THE PEACE OF GOD
4.1-13

The Author now brings to a conclusion his parallel of the double Exodus by comparing the 'REST' which the Psalmist spoke of, which meant for Israel an end to their desert wanderings and a fixed home in Canaan, the Land of the Promise, with the final 'REST' which awaits the People of God after their earthly pilgrimage, the peace and fellowship of God. His argument runs as follows: God created the world in six days and rested on the seventh. For God, therefore, existence now is a perpetual sabbath-peace. Christians will share that SABBATH-REST if they are faithful to their calling. The people of Israel were called too and the good news of God's Rest was proclaimed to them. It was available to them from the beginning but they could not grasp it because of their lack of faith. The Rest that they hoped for in Canaan was likewise denied them for forty years because of their lack of faith. Once more after that disciplinary period the chance of entering what they thought was God's Rest came again under Joshua. They took possession of the Holy Land and settled there. But they were mistaken in thinking that that was what God meant by his REST. What they found in Canaan was merely an end to their wanderings. And did not God much later than Joshua's day say through the Psalmist David that the offer of entering the Rest of God was still open to-day? That means that the offer is open even now.

CHRISTIAN REST

The Author's scholastic exegesis and his questionable

51

views on the origin of the Psalter should not disguise from us his main theme which is still valid. The peace which comes from the perfect relationship with God, of which the peace and worship of the seventh day are or should be a foretaste, is the goal of the Christian life. It is not the end of activity but the end of all futile striving, in uninterrupted fellowship with God. Through Christ we may begin to share that experience here and now and recognize in Moses, Joshua and the Psalmist sign-posts pointing to him.

SEPARATIST TENDENCIES?

A special reference to the situation of the readers may be contained in v. 2 where the lack of trust in God on the part of Israel is condemned. Not all failed to profit by the words that God spoke to them, but only those who were NOT UNITED BY FAITH with their leaders. Is this an allusion to a group of Christians in Rome whose yearning for the security that they had known in Judaism tended to make them separate themselves from the main body of the Church there?

12-13. the word of God

Having warned his readers against the disobedience which deprived Israel of entrance into the true Rest of God, the Author concludes this prologue to his main theme with a striking description of the power of the Word of God in Christ to search out the chinks in our armour. In words which reflect both Philo and the Book of Wisdom, he reaches a conception which is however far from speculative. God's Word is living, active, piercing, discerning. We stand constantly confronted by it, under its judgement. We can have no inner secrets of heart or mind from HIM WITH WHOM WE HAVE TO DO (i.e. reckon).

OUR GREAT HIGH PRIEST
4.14-16

The Author now begins the main section of his letter, which deals with the nature of the High Priesthood of Jesus. In the next and subsequent chapters he will show in detail that what the Jewish High Priest was unable to do for men Jesus can do, and will contrast the perfect self-offering of Jesus with the imperfection of the Jewish sacrificial system. Meanwhile he gives us in a few sentences what is in effect a summary of what he has already said in different connections, focusing it now on the one theme which he is about to develop.

Since, he says, we have a great High Priest who has PASSED THROUGH THE HEAVENS, i.e. who is now at the very Throne of God, let us stand by our confession of faith. Our great High Priest is Jesus, the Son of God: the man of Nazareth who was God incarnate. For what do we mean by High Priesthood? What did the Jews expect from their High Priest? Surely it was man's attempt to get right with God, to be at one with him, to bridge the gulf that separated guilty consciences and sinful habits from the holiness of God. If the gulf is to be bridged it must be by one who is able to enter into all human weaknesses and understand all human failings. The Jewish High Priest could do this because he was a sinful man like his neighbours. He could therefore sympathize with human weakness and failure. But he could do no more. He could not help them. Only one who himself knew all the temptations of human life and yet resisted them to the uttermost could not only sympathize but stretch out his hand to his weaker brothers and lift them up.

Jesus alone was able to do both. He was (lit.) TEMPTED IN ALL RESPECTS ACCORDING TO (HIS) LIKENESS (WITH US, YET) WITHOUT SIN. This would not of course mean that every sort of human temptation was felt by Jesus, for some of our temptations are the result of our own sin, and Jesus was WITHOUT SIN. Nor would it mean that the particular forms that temptation takes in different spheres of experience would present themselves in all their variety to Jesus. The temptation to rob a bank or betray atomic secrets would obviously not present itself to Jesus in that form. Saints however have their own temptations, less blatant but felt more keenly. His temptations would be those of a first century Jew, but of a highly sensitive Jew who felt that he had a power that no one else shared, which he could either use to the glory of God or devote to the basest ends.

In this sense, and in view of the depth and range of Jesus' personality, it would be true to say that his temptation was far greater than that of ordinary mortals. There are limits to the evil that most of us can do because of the limits of our power. There was no limit to the evil Jesus could have done had he chosen the KINGDOMS OF THE WORLD instead of the service of God (Matt. 4.8f.).

Most of us, too, succumb easily to our temptations. Jesus, however, never once betrayed any sign of a guilty conscience, any sense of separation from God or wavering of obedience. To achieve that result meant that the struggle must have been of an intensity unknown to any other man.

The Author would have nothing to do with any suggestion that Jesus was naturally good, or that he started with an unfair advantage. If we had questioned him closely he would no doubt have said that the Incarnation involved necessary limitation; limitation of knowledge, except the knowledge of God; limitation of power, except the power that comes from that perfect knowledge. He would have added that God having given us all freedom to choose right or wrong, all men have always chosen some things wrong, except Christ. His sympathy and understanding and efficacy as a High Priest came from his triumphant victory over the sins that defeat the rest of us. The courage and mastery of the Leader give his followers new heart.

But since Jesus is God expressed in human terms, God come into human experience, it means that what we say about Jesus we are saying about God. Because we know that Jesus experienced temptation we know that God is able to understand the follies of men and to forgive them. For forgiveness is essentially entering the experience of the person who wrongs us, knowing why he did it and understanding his motives. Our Christian faith is that we do not rely on man-made attempts to bridge the gulf to God, for God has bridged it for us through his Son. He has provided the At-one-ment by entering into our life and bearing our sins for us.

Therefore we may with BOLDNESS, or confidence, approach the THRONE OF GRACE knowing that God understands, and knowing that we shall receive MERCY, i.e. forgiveness, and GRACE, or power, to resist our temptations IN TIME OF NEED.

NOTE ON THE FUNCTIONS OF A HIGH PRIEST

Jesus has been proclaimed as the High Priest who supersedes all others, and something has been said about his qualifications for the office. Now the Author, assuming that his readers know what he is talking about, contrasts in more detail High Priesthood under the old dispensation with the High Priesthood of Christ. It is time for us therefore, not having such background knowledge ourselves, to look at the practice and purpose of the High Priestly office as it existed at the time of Christ.

THE LAW

The Jewish state, although technically part of the Roman Empire, was a theocracy. Its life was controlled and regulated by religious laws. From the beginning the Jews had thought of themselves as the People of God, since he had at the Exodus singled them out from among all the tribes and countries of the world, to receive his revelation of himself and to be his witnesses among the nations. Their community life was therefore an attempt to exemplify how a God-fearing people should behave. The Torah or Law, which had grown on the foundation of the Ten Commandments enunciated by Moses, included by the time of Christ not only the basic provisions as contained in the Old Testament, but also a vast mass of legislation which, in the course of time, had been added by way of clarification, and to provide for all exigencies.

THE TWO ASPECTS OF THE LAW

In this great body of regulations there was no distinction made between sacred and secular, civil or religious affairs. The Jews would not have acknowledged that there was any difference. Public sanitation and the service of the altar were both equally governed by the Law of God. In practice, however, a distinction was made in respect of those aspects of the life of the community which were directly concerned with the worship of God (although in a sense ideally the whole of life was regarded as worship). Roughly speaking it was the distinction between the Temple at Jerusalem, and the rules for all that went on there, and the daily life of the people which was regulated by the synagogues where the Law was taught and expounded.

THE TEMPLE

The Temple was the traditional centre of national religion, where the ancient symbols of the Exodus had been enshrined, the Ark of the Covenant with the stone tablets of the Decalogue, and where still its series of outer and inner courts led up to the little chapel called the Holy of Holies, where stood the Mercy-seat, symbolic of the Throne of the unseen God. To maintain the services of the Temple, and the vast traffic in animal sacrifice that went on there, a veritable army of priests and attendants was employed. All their activities, their dress and their functions were carefully laid down in the text of the Law.

THE HIGH PRIEST

From the ranks of the ordinary priesthood, in the course of the centuries, had emerged the office of High Priest. It was inevitable in such a theocratic community, that when the kings, who had been regarded as God's representatives, became progressively ineffective and corrupt, people looked to the priesthood to provide the necessary leadership. Even before the Exile, with such an outstandingly God-fearing king as Josiah, the place of Hilkiah in the state was no mean one (II Kings 22-23). After the Exile, however, there was no question but that the High Priest became the civic and religious leader of the community. During the Maccabean period in the second century B.C. the office became almost synonymous with kingship and attracted many of the worst characters in Jewish history.

THE TEMPLE AT THE TIME OF CHRIST

In New Testament times, as can be seen from the Gospel narratives, High Priests such as Annas and Caiaphas wielded considerable power even indirectly over their nominal master, the Roman procurator. The equivocal position, however, of the priestly party, the Sadducees, in relation to the Imperial government, and the unsavoury history of the High Priests themselves meant that in popular esteem moral authority and spiritual leadership were looked for rather from the Pharisees, the legal and theological experts among the laity. Yet although the synagogue had more influence on the life of the people, the Temple and its worship were part of the warp and woof of the Jewish faith, attracting the allegiance and devotion of Jews everywhere, whether in

Palestine or overseas. Its ministrations fulfilled a function
that nothing could replace. Similarly the High Priest, whatever his personal failings or political reputation may have
been, occupied a role on the religious side which was unique.

THE DAY OF ATONEMENT

Although for the rest of the year as priest his office was
no more significant than that of his Temple colleagues, on
one day the function of the High Priest was supreme. This
was the Day of Atonement (*Yom Kippur*), commonly known
as *the* Day (*Yoma*), which is still observed and hallowed
above all others by world Jewry. On this day, until the
Temple was finally destroyed in A.D. 70, the High Priest
entered the Holy of Holies to make atonement in the
presence of God for the sins of the nation. He was the
unique mediator who represented the people before God and
sought to bridge the gulf between a Holy God and a sinful
community.

SINS OF IGNORANCE

It should be emphasized that the sins he atoned for were
not the wilful transgressions of the Law; murder, adultery,
theft, sabbath-breaking and crimes of that kind. These
were punishable—and were punished—under the ordinary
provisions of the Law. The Day of Atonement on the other
hand was principally designed to cover the sins that had
been committed unwittingly, through ignorance or omission,
in the course of the preceding year by society as a whole.
It was fundamentally a wholesome recognition that no man
is or can be sinless. Even the most punctilious Pharisee,
for all his prayers and fasting, and meticulous observance
of the letter of the Law, could not fulfil God's demands. As
a token of this the High Priest himself, as his first act in
the ritual, made an offering for his own sins and the sins of
the priesthood.

THE RITUAL

The Day of Atonement was celebrated on the tenth day of the seventh month as a day of complete rest, fasting and penitence. The ritual is described in Lev. 16, and in the Mishna, the written interpretation of the Torah which had grown up over the few hundred years since the Law was finally codified. According to this the High Priest first discarded his normal vestments, bathed, and put on a white robe. He then killed a bullock which was to be a sin-offering for himself and his associates, entered alone the Holy of Holies, and having censed it, sprinkled the blood of the bullock around the Mercy-seat.

Having done this he returned to the people, who had provided two goats. One of them he selected for God and the other for Azazel, the demon of the wilderness, who was symbolic of evil. The goat dedicated to God was killed by the High Priest, who returned into the Holy of Holies and sprinkled its blood in the same place as that of the bullock. He then sprinkled the blood of both goat and bullock on the altar outside, where normally the daily animal sacrifices were made. This done he performed the most striking action of the ritual. Placing his hands on the living goat, he confessed over it the sins which Israel had committed during the past year and prayed for God's forgiveness. The goat was then led away into the desert and destroyed.

THE MEANING BEHIND IT

Twentieth century Anglo-Saxon humanitarianism must not cause us to dismiss all this as a revolting travesty of the worship of God and to denounce High Priesthood—or indeed all priesthood in those days—as holy butchery. To us it is a ghastly performance, but before we become too self-righteous about the killing of helpless animals let us remember how recent is our humanitarianism, and let us reflect on the unholy butchery of helpless children on our roads every year, which is certainly more of a crime against God's creatures than animal sacrifice. Those who practised that at least thought that they were acting in accordance with the will of God. What they would have said about Hiroshima or Nagasaki can be imagined.

The High Priest was doing something on behalf of God in relation to the people, and doing something on behalf of the people in relation to God. It was the attempt of a sinful High Priest to effect an at-one-ment between God and a sinful people including himself, by taking the burden of their sins from off their shoulders and placing it upon the shoulders of a recognized representative divinely sanctioned. By sacrificing the bullock and the goat and sprinkling their blood on the holy places symbolic of the presence of God, it was believed that the life of the animals contained in their blood united both parties in the transaction. The neutral third party bridged the gulf between the other two. Similarly by sending the goat into the wilderness the people symbolically sent their sins with it to the demon world where they belonged.

THE MEDIATOR

The High Priest was thus primarily a mediator between God and the people. The means he used were those which according to the mind of the times in which he lived seemed to be most appropriate. The prophets had grandly exhorted men to do justly, love mercy and walk humbly with God (Mic. 6.8). The whole animal sacrificial system, including the Day of Atonement, whatever its inadequacies, was an honest recognition that the prophetic standard was unattainable, and that without some kind of third party intervention the end of men's striving was frustration and despair. In particular the office of High Priest and the symbolism of the ritual of the Day of Atonement pointed directly to the need for such mediation as the Gospel claimed to provide.

V

THE QUALIFICATIONS OF A HIGH PRIEST
5.1-10

In view of the vital role which the High Priest has to play it is essential that so important a mediator between God and man should be in the first place called by God and not self-appointed. In the second place he must understand human frailty in order to be able to intercede for others. According to the Author, Jewish practice was satisfactory on both counts. Aaron, who was of the tribe of Levi, was set apart by God for the priesthood (Ex. 28.1), and according to the Law it was only by his descendants that all priestly activities could be carried out. The office was thus tantamount to a call from God in that the levitical succession was secure from human intervention. In this respect the Author saw too rosy a picture. The Aaronic succession was in fact very dubious, and the priesthood had only within the last few hundred years been concentrated in levitical hands. Before that, a member of any tribe might be consecrated priest. His second requirement was however certainly satisfied in that the High Priest understood human frailty so well that he made atonement for his own sins before anyone else's (vv. 1-4).

A UNIQUE CALL

We are now shown how Jesus fulfilled both these conditions more perfectly than any purely human High Priest could do. In defence of the claim that Jesus was not self-appointed, but was called to the office by God, the Author

cites two Old Testament texts. The first is from the
Messianic Ps. 2.7, and has already been used in 1.5 in
another connection: THOU ART MY SON, THIS DAY HAVE I
BEGOTTEN THEE. This does not mean that before 'this day'
Christ was non-existent, any more than it does in the
previous use of the quotation where it follows an assertion
that Christ was co-eternal with God (1.2). The Author uses
his Old Testament with imagination and not with the
callipers of the literalist. He takes out of this quotation the
meaning 'This day I have appointed thee' and treats it, as
in the case of Aaron, as a divine call. In so doing he was
following our Lord himself, who had used these very words
to describe his baptismal experience (Mark 1.9-11).

A UNIQUE PRIESTHOOD

His second quotation is again from a Messianic Psalm,
110.4: THOU ART A PRIEST FOREVER AFTER THE ORDER OF
MELCHIZEDEK. As we have seen (note on 3.1) there is no
reason to suppose that the Author was the first in Christian
circles to connect the High Priestly idea with the Messiah.
Part of the Jewish Messianic expectation was centred on one
who would be an Aaronite. It was natural for those connected with the priesthood to look for a Son of Levi instead
of sharing the more usual expectation of a Son of David.
The point of the quotation is that since Melchizedek, of
whom we shall hear more in chapter 7, was contemporary
with Abraham, his priesthood had higher standing than that
of Aaron, whose ancestor Levi came three generations later.
The High Priesthood of Jesus, which as scripture attested
was of THE ORDER OF MELCHIZEDEK, was therefore clearly
superior to that of any Levite (vv. 5-6).

A UNIQUE EXPERIENCE

The Author now turns to the second condition of High
Priesthood, that he must sympathize with human weakness.

This, he says, Jesus could perfectly do, not because he had
sinned himself, but because he had suffered to the uttermost.
Indeed he LEARNED OBEDIENCE BY THE THINGS WHICH HE
SUFFERED. This might seem to mean that Jesus learned
obedience only through suffering, as if he found by experience that obedience paid better than disobedience. The
Author means something quite different. What Jesus learned
by bitter experience was that true obedience entails suffering.
There is no escaping the penalties of the service of God. In
order therefore to be perfect man, the pattern of true sonship, Jesus had to experience what such sonship involves.
He had to pay the price in pain of body and anguish of mind,
but having touched the depths of human sorrow he is able
to lead his brethren to God. He might have expected to
be free of suffering since he was a SON, but it was necessary
if he was to be THE AUTHOR OF SALVATION (2.10) for all other
sons.

THE AGONY OF JESUS

Gethsemane is taken to be the point of the deepest human
experience of Jesus, and the Author takes it for granted that
his readers know the details of Jesus's earthly ministry. The
physical agony of the Cross was not so crushing as his agony
of spirit in the Garden. His cries and tears there (which are
not mentioned in the Gospel narrative) was caused not by
the horror of death but by the horror of evil, the recognition
of the barrier it erected between God and man. Jesus tasted
to the full there the depths to which human envy and
prejudice and bigotry could bring men down, and bore the
whole tragedy of the human situation in his own spirit. This
was perhaps, in the Author's mind, the sacrifice of Christ on
his own behalf, which corresponded with the offering of the
High Priest in the Temple. And he was HEARD although the
answer to his prayer that the cup might pass from him was:
'No!' He was heard in the sense that he was given such
perfect communion with God as enabled him to say: 'Not

my will but thy will be done.' This was his reverence or
GODLY FEAR. Who then had more right to be NAMED OF
GOD A HIGH PRIEST AFTER THE ORDER OF MELCHIZEDEK
(vv. 7-10)?

THE IMPATIENCE OF AN AUTHOR
5.11-14

From 5.11 to 6.20 there is a lengthy digression before the
Author returns to the theme of High Priesthood. He seems
to feel that he has been in a sense talking over the heads of
his readers, for he breaks off his argument to complain
about their obtuseness (v. 11). Considering the length of
time they have been enrolled in the membership of the
Church they are disappointingly immature. They ought by
now to be in a position to instruct others in the faith, instead
of which they are still at the ABC stage themselves (v. 12).
They ought to be able to take the strong meat of the full
Gospel instead of a kind of milk and water diet of Christianity. It is time they grew up (vv. 13-14). They must
make up their minds to become fully grown Christians, and
not remain for ever at the kindergarten level (6.1).

THE IMPLICATIONS OF THE GOSPEL

Various commentators explain these verses differently.
It is suggested, for example, that the Author wants his
readers to use their intellectual powers more than they have
been doing, and to advance to higher levels of theological
speculation. Another suggestion is that he is urging them
in the Alexandrian manner to press on to the ideal. Or
again that the elements of the Gospel are childish and must
be left behind. None of these seems as likely as that the
Author's concern is aroused primarily because his readers
are failing to realize the full implications of the Gospel to
which they are committed. They are called to action for

Christ in the world, instead of which they seem to be little
farther on in their understanding of what it means to be
committed Christians than when they started. Must we,
says the Author, begin all over again explaining what our
faith involves?

E

VI

CHRISTIAN FOUNDATIONS
6.1-2

In vv. 1-2 the Author lists some of the fundamental features of the Gospel, which look like the contents of a primitive catechism. These are of interest in that they indicate the themes of missionary preaching at a very early stage in Christianity, and also in that they are without exception also features of Jewish faith and practice. It would therefore be more difficult for people to whom these doctrines were already familiar to appreciate their new Christian content than for pagans who met them for the first time. The items which are cited as foundation stones embrace the Christian attitude to the Law, to Faith, to Baptism, to Resurrection and to Judgement. The Author implies that if his readers understood these doctrines properly they would show signs of measuring up better to what was expected of them.

REPENTANCE AND FAITH

The Christian Faith involves, first of all, REPENTANCE. This is fundamental. It means a change of heart and mind, a redirection of the whole personality: turning our backs on our past sins, or perhaps Pharisaic legalism, and recognizing that they are DEAD WORKS. The sequel to repentance is FAITH IN GOD, committing our lives to him as we know him in Jesus Christ in complete trust and confidence: becoming God-centred instead of self-centred. This is the first step in Christianity. Jesus called it being born again or recovering the childlike heart (John 3.3; Mark 10.15).

BAPTISM

The second step is admission into the Church and the obligations which that involves. BAPTISM was a common initiation ceremony, both in pagan Mystery Religions and in Judaism. But for Christians it was the symbol of entrance into the membership of the Body of Christ and the assumption of the responsibilities attaching to a member of the People of God. The sequel to that was in early Church practice the LAYING ON OF HANDS. This was the mark of the gift of the Holy Spirit, at first, as we have seen (note on 2.4), closely associated with the ecstatic 'gift of tongues' (Acts 8.17-19; 19.6), but even then also recognized as symbolizing the new quality of life that came from the presence of Christ among his people.

RESURRECTION AND JUDGEMENT

If we call the first pair of propositions in this early Christian catechism doctrinal and the second pair sacramental, we should have to call the third and last pair eschatological, since they deal with what happens beyond life as we know it. RESURRECTION and JUDGEMENT were part of the carry-over from Jewish to Christian belief. The germs of both ideas are in the Old Testament, but it was in the inter-testamental period that they reached their full development. The Greek view of the relationship of body and soul made any thought of resurrection ridiculous (cf. Acts 17.32). The soul was the body's prisoner, and at death it was set free. The immortality of the soul was however never a biblical doctrine. The Jews believed that body and soul were inseparable, that man was a unity. Modern medicine, be it noted, also speaks of man as a psychosomatic organism. The biblical view was that if there were any life beyond death it must involve the whole man, with his total personality, in which his body, however transformed, must play a part.

THE CHRISTIAN VIEW

The doctrine which developed in the period between the Testaments was, broadly speaking, that when Messiah came there would be a general resurrection of the dead, followed by divine judgement, when those who had merited it would receive the reward of everlasting life, and those who had deserved punishment would suffer correspondingly. By and large this view was adopted by the early Church. The main difference for Christians was that by the Resurrection of Jesus they had certain knowledge that they would share eternal life with him and that the Judge would be the Christ himself. Behind this mythological framework, however, lay the heart of the matter, that the believer united to his Lord in personal commitment would share his victory over death, and that the ultimate criterion of eternal union with God or eternal separation from him was a man's response to his encounter with Christ. In this sense he stood from that moment under his Judgement.

NO EUCHARIST?

Two points of interest arise from this catechism. The first is that among the fundamental beliefs there is no mention of the Eucharist. It might have been expected that such a vital and distinctive feature of early Christian worship would have been associated with baptism. It may be, however, that since the Author is obviously not trying to exhaust the whole range of Christian teaching in his ABC of Christianity, he has selected those points which for his purpose most needed emphasis, as marking the difference between the Jewish and Christian attitude to their religious obligations, and meeting the immediate needs of his readers. If the epistle is rightly regarded as a summons to go forth into the world in faith, the LAYING ON OF HANDS, signifying the living power of the Spirit, would be most appropriate. Equally relevant would be the mention of the Christian hope of RESURRECTION to people facing persecution.

APOLLOS?

The second minor point is that the odd plural use of the word 'baptism' may simply refer to the contrast between Jewish and Christian baptism, but it might also be accounted for if Apollos was the Author, since according to Acts 18.25–19.7 he reckoned the 'repentance baptism' of John the Baptist to be adequate for Christians, until he was taken in hand by the learned Priscilla and her husband.

DISCUSSION OR ACTION

We might reflect on this whole section, and the impatience of the Author, that the inclination to stop short at the fundamentals is not confined to his readers. It is a perennial temptation in Christian circles, especially when the outside world and its affairs seem to be more chaotic than usual, to take refuge in theological discussion and allege that the primary need is for Christians to know their foundations, whether doctrinal or biblical. 'Back to the Creeds' or 'Back to the Bible' may well be a form of escapism from the task of carrying the Christian message actively into the world around. The Author at all events would seem to suggest that if we wait until we think we know the fundamentals of our faith we are failing to take the risks and face the dangers of the kind of frontier action to which the Gospel summons us.

NO SECOND CHANCE
6.3-8

So, says the Author, with the help of God let us take the elementary facts of our faith as read and press on to matters which ought to concern grown-up Christians (v. 3). Whereupon he proceeds to utter a dire warning against backsliders, and appears to assert that for them there will be no second chance. This passage has been favourably commended by rigorists from Tertullian onwards, and has been cited as

scriptural authority for denying the possibility of returning
to the fellowship of the Church after once leaving it.

APOSTASY

Let us however assume the situation to be that the Author
is speaking of the young Christian community in Rome on
the eve of the Neronian persecution.   There indeed they
were called on to think maturely, to make decisions from
day to day, to live on a knife-edge.   There was no place
there for ABC Christians who busied themselves with
doctrinal problems, but for men and women of action who
were prepared to take the consequences of carrying the
Gospel into the open.   Such people would not be deterred
by fear of death.   Doubtless some had already renounced
their Christian faith and embraced paganism.   This meant
literally cursing Christ blasphemously and irrevocably.
Deliberate apostasy of this order, says the Author, can have
no forgiveness.   He is thus speaking of no mere moral lapse
or even moral breakdown, for what Christian has ever
avoided these in some measure?   The whole epistle
proclaims a God who understands human weakness and,
because he understands, forgives.

SECOND CRUCIFIXION

But here is a situation where a man has been ENLIGH-
TENED, has seen 'the light of the knowledge of the glory of
God in the face of Jesus Christ' (II Cor. 4.6) and has com-
mitted himself to him.   He has TASTED OF THE HEAVENLY
GIFT, that is, has known the love of God.   He has been a
PARTAKER OF THE HOLY GHOST in that he has experienced the
power of the Spirit of God in his daily life.   He has TASTED
THE GOOD WORD OF GOD by satisfying himself that his faith is
grounded on history and supported by reason, and he has
lived already in a new dimension, sharing THE POWER OF
THE AGE TO COME.   If after all that, says the Author, a man
can renounce Christ and curse him, he is finished.   This

amounts to CRUCIFYING THE SON OF GOD AFRESH and holding
him up to contempt before the whole world. It is like a
field which has had every chance and produces a good crop.
Such land receives God's blessing. If it sprouts THORNS AND
THISTLES, however, there is nothing for it but to burn them
up.

The Author may be right, or it may be that in his earnest
conviction of the necessity for the Church to hold out against
what amounted to a threat of extermination, he under-
estimated the mercy of God, who knows the complexities
of the choices men have to make better than their fellows.
Faced with Nazism or Communism many pastors and lay-
men have refused to barter their convictions for their lives
and have paid the price, to the greater glory of God and the
credit and expansion of his Church. Many on the other
hand have believed that there are other ways of witnessing
for their faith in these circumstances, and who but God, who
knows the secrets of men's hearts, can stand in judgement
on them?

GROUNDS FOR HOPE
6.9-12

Within the circle, however, to which the Author is writing,
no such apostasy has occurred, and he believes that none
will. His concern for them seems therefore to be their lack
of courage and adventure generally, their failure to see the
wider issues. If the testing time came for them they would
be less likely to put up resistance if they had been living in
a little backwater, than if the quality of their faith showed
more intensity and expectancy. The Author believes in the
maxim that those who do not go forward are likely to go
back.

He has confidence, however, that they will ultimately
justify his faith in them for two reasons: first, because of
the help they have given their fellow Christians in the past,
which probably is an allusion to the persecution referred

to in 10.32-34. This type of brotherly service they are still
providing, showing that they have the true spirit of Christ.
The second reason for the Author's confidence that they will
not fail is that God will not forget their good work. This
does not mean that God would be prepared to overlook
apostasy for the sake of their past service, but rather that
by their service they have made themselves fitter to resist
the temptation to apostatize.

So the Author urges them to keep up this spirit and extend
it to every part of their Christian life. They are not to be
content with MINISTERING TO THE SAINTS, but are to carry
that same outward-looking concern to its uttermost limits,
imitating those who by their FAITH and PATIENCE experience
already the foretaste of the promised perfect union with
God. We shall hear more of these witnesses for Christ in
chapters 11-12.

THE ANCHOR OF THE SOUL
6.13-20

Meantime the word PROMISES in the last sentence attracts
the Author's attention for a moment before he resumes the
main theme which he left at 5.10. The ' promise ' of God is,
of course, that of eternal life; life in his presence for his
faithful people; the consummation of all Christian experience and the content of Christian hope. The Author has
elsewhere referred to it as REST (4.9) and GLORY (2.10). But
now he shows its true scope.

God, he says, has not only promised but has given his
oath that he will fulfil the promise. When Abraham showed
by a supreme act of faith that he was willing, if God
demanded it, to offer up Isaac his only son, God not only
promised him a blessing as a reward for his perfect obedience and steadfastness, but to make it doubly sure he con-
firmed it by oath. The reference is to Gen. 22.16-18: BY
MYSELF HAVE I SWORN, SAITH THE LORD . . . IN THY SEED
SHALL ALL THE NATIONS OF THE EARTH BE BLESSED. From

the point of view of the Author and his readers an oath was inviolable. The casual perjuries of present-day law courts were unheard of among these backward people, for whose simple minds the name of God had still some meaning. For God to swear by himself meant that no promise could ever be more binding.

But the promise to Abraham was a promise to the Christian Church, for through the Messiah, the New Israel had inherited the blessing given to Abraham, whose spiritual descendants they were. The full promise then is that the world would be brought back to God, and its people restored to the perfect realization of sonship. *Through* the Church this would happen, and *in* the Church it had begun to happen. The fulfilment of this hope is what lies before us, beset as we are on every hand. It is an anchor, SURE AND STEDFAST in the stormy seas of life. It reaches through the VEIL which hides from our view the unseen realm of God, which we yet can glimpse here and now, and in which we believe through Jesus Christ. For he, our great High Priest, has already pierced the veil, paving the way for us to follow. Thus through him we and all his people shall reach the fulfilment of the promise in God's presence.

With the reference to the VEIL the Author has now come back full circle to the High Priesthood of Jesus. In the Temple at Jerusalem (or the Tabernacle of the Exodus which the Author prefers to cite) there were in the inmost sanctuary two chambers: the Holy Place, and beyond it, separated from it by a curtain or 'veil', the Holy of Holies, which was the symbolic Presence of God. On the Day of Atonement the High Priest passed through the 'veil' when he entered God's Presence on behalf of the people, following the command to Aaron in Lev. 16. But the Holy of Holies in Jerusalem was but the shadow of the real Presence of God. Jesus, the true High Priest, has now passed through the 'veil' to the veritable Throne of Grace, as a FORE-RUNNER, or PIONEER, to lead his people to God.

VII

MELCHIZEDEK
7.1-3

IN GENESIS 14

We are treated now to a fantastic piece of speculation, which, though it was entirely in line with Alexandrian Judaism at that time, carries no conviction to-day. The author wishes to show that Melchizedek, whom he has already mentioned on several occasions, was a priest of a different type from all others, and that he was the prototype of Jesus. In order to do this he reads into the scanty reference to this enigmatic personage in Gen. 14.18-20 a variety of dubious meanings. Presumably there is some historical substance in that odd chapter of Genesis which is sandwiched into a straightforward narrative of Abraham's career, and transforms him for a brief space from a peaceful nomad into a warrior chieftain. The narrative records that after his victorious return from the problematical Battle of the Kings, Abraham was blessed by Melchizedek, Priest-King of Jerusalem, who regaled him with bread and wine, and received a tenth of the spoils of war. It is quite conceivable that the chieftain of the powerful stronghold of Jerusalem, then called Uru-Salim, which remained in enemy hands for a thousand years after Abraham's day, was in a position to exact tribute, and that the Genesis narrative dating from the time of the monarchy is designed to establish the historic right of the Jerusalem priesthood to tithes.

IN PSALM 110

The incident was taken up by the writer of Ps. 110, who included among the attributes of God's Anointed that he should be a priest for ever with the rank of Melchizedek. At one time it was thought that this psalm was of Maccabean origin and referred to Simon Maccabeus, the Priest-King of the second century B.C. More recently it has been taken to date from the period of the monarchy several hundred years earlier, and to refer to David or some later king, who is spoken of as the Lord's Anointed. The psalm itself might be part of the ritual of a Royal Enthronement. Melchizedek who, if historical, must have been a Jebusite chief, since Jerusalem was in the hands of that tribe until David's day (II Sam. 5.4-10), would naturally feature in the psalm since the attributes of the former rulers of Jerusalem would pertain to David and his successors after its capture. The king of Israel, who was Yahweh's Anointed, would therefore properly be described as a priest for ever of the order of Melchizedek. What applied to the king applied *a fortiori* to the Anointed King who was the object of Jewish hope when native kingship had given place to the domination of world empires. When he came he would sum up in himself all the attributes that were proper to God's representative.

IN HEBREWS

While the Psalmist contented himself with briefly relating the Priest-King of Salem to the subject of his psalm, the Author goes further and allegorizes the whole incident as Messianic. He picks out five points from the narrative as of deep significance: (1) that Melchizedek was King of Jerusalem, (2) that he was Priest of the Most High God, (3) that he blessed Abraham, (4) that he received tithe from him, and (5) that, unlike most Old Testament characters, his parentage is not given. Messianic significance is also seen in the fact that Melchizedek's name in Hebrew means 'King of Righteousness', and that Salem means 'peace'. Is not Messiah called Prince of Peace by the prophet Isaiah (9.6), and is it not said that in the Age to Come Righteousness and Peace will kiss each other (Ps. 85.10)? Moreover, the fact that no genealogy is supplied in the case of Melchizedek surely implies a unique type of priesthood, since he has apparently no father or mother, to say nothing of no beginning or end to his life. He was therefore a foreshadowing of Jesus who between his pre-existence with God and his present exaltation with God appeared suddenly on earth for a brief space like this mysterious Priest of Salem and may be regarded as his fulfilment.

In fairness to the Author it should be said that this fantasy is more restrained than the allegorical speculations of the Christian Fathers, or their present day disciples, whose imaginations know no bounds in discerning Christian meanings in Old Testament incidents, even to seeing in Melchizedek's offer of bread and wine a foreshadowing of the Eucharist. The Author spares us that. Further he does not regard Jesus as literally fulfilling the type of Melchizedek (the absence of whose parentage probably means that it was unknown, or simply springs from the fact that the incident is recorded in the Jahwist source of Genesis, which was less concerned with genealogies than the priestly source), because he later refers to Jesus as of the tribe of Judah (v. 14), and no Christian teaching has ever suggested that Jesus was motherless. Nor can he be expected to have known that the Hebrew for Most High God was El Elyon, who was probably the chief god of Canaanite mythology, or that Melchizedek more likely means: ' My king is Sidiq,' which was the name of a god.

THE SUPERIORITY OF MELCHIZEDEK
7.4-10

So he proceeds undaunted to prove the superiority of Melchizedek over the orthodox Jewish priesthood. Melchizedek is immortal, since we are not told that he ever died, whereas ordinary priests unquestionably do. Further he blessed Abraham, and in so doing showed that he possessed greater authority than the Father of Israel who had received the Promise, since it is always the possessor of greater power who communicates it in blessing to the recipient. In addition he exacted tribute of a tithe of the spoils that Abraham had won. Now the fact that the levitical priests are entitled by law to tithes from the common people puts them on a higher level than ordinary men. So therefore the exaction of a tithe from Abraham puts Melchizedek above all the priesthood, since all priests are the descendants of Abraham, including Levi the founder of the priestly caste. In a sense Levi, yet unborn, shared in the action of his great ancestor, as the members of the levitical priesthood shared in the commitments of their founder.

THE END OF THE LAW
7.11-17

But supposing someone were to say: That may well be so, but has not the Aaronic priesthood superseded that of Melchizedek? The answer to that is that the Melchizedek priesthood existed before the Aaronic priesthood, and the Psalmist spoke of the Messiah as a Melchizedek priest. Therefore the Melchizedek priesthood had been dormant while the Aaronic priesthood held sway. If the Aaronic priesthood has been adequate to bridge the gulf between man and God there would have been no need of such a Priest as the Psalmist foretold. Consequently whenever the Psalmist's Messianic prophecy was fulfilled the Aaronic priesthood must have come to an end, and similarly the Law which established it. The proof of this is that Jesus, who is undoubtedly the true Priest, is not a Levite at all but, being Son of David, is of the tribe of Judah. Since the Law laid it down that only Levites might be priests it was obviously now abrogated. Jesus' claim to Priesthood rests on something greater than the Law, namely his indestructible life.

THE END OF THE COVENANT
7.18-25

The real weakness of the Law, however, was that it utterly
failed to achieve what was in fact its major purpose, to put
men into the right relationship with God. The daily practice
of priestly sacrifice in the Temple, together with the acts of
the High Priest on the Day of Atonement, could not ease a
guilty conscience or restore the broken fellowship with God.
THE LAW MADE NOTHING PERFECT. Therefore God has
replaced the Law with a new and BETTER HOPE which made
possible a new relationship between himself and man. The
old type of priesthood inherited their office by the automatic
process of belonging to the levitical caste, but this new
type of priesthood, affirmed by God's oath (Ps. 110.4), con-
stitutes a New Covenant. This new partnership with God
had been heralded by the prophet Jeremiah (31.31f.) as one
which would supersede the Old Covenant of Sinai embodied
in the written Law, and would be based on a direct personal
fellowship between God and his people, including the forgiveness of their sins. At his death Jesus had announced
that this New Covenant was established through him. He
is thus the guarantee that it has come into being. Such a
new relationship between God and man is now possible
because we do not depend on a chain of High Priests which
is broken by death, but on one High Priest who is able to
save completely from their sins by his eternal pleading all
who approach God through him. We are to hear more of
this in chapters 9 and 10.

ONCE AND FOR ALL
7.26-28

In the last few verses the Author summarizes what he has
been saying and raises other points which he will develop

later. The true High Priest, he says, had to be different
from the rest, holy, innocent, unstained, removed from all
contact with sinners, exalted to the Throne of God. Here
the contrast is between the ritual cleanness which was demanded of the High Priest and the personal sanctity of
Jesus. There is also an allusion to the fact that the High
Priest remained apart from human contact for seven days
before the Day of Atonement, whereas Jesus is eternally
with God. Unlike the others he had no need to offer daily
sacrifices to atone for his own and the people's sins. On
the contrary he did this once and for all when he offered
up himself. According to the Law, the High Priest was a
fallible mortal, but according to God's oath, which superseded it, his Son is the true High Priest made perfect through
his suffering for evermore.

It should be noted that the author tends to use the words
priest and High Priest as synonyms. Thus although Melchizedek is according to the scriptural reference a priest,
and Jesus is held to be comparable to him, it is with the
specific activity of the High Priest on the Day of Atonement
that the Author is concerned. Likewise the reference to
High Priests offering up daily sacrifices is strictly incorrect
since these were offered by any priest and were not sin-
offerings, whereas the High Priest as such sacrificed FOR THE
SINS OF THE PEOPLE only on the Day of Atonement.

This laborious effort to prove from scripture that the
Priesthood, Law, and Covenant of the old regime have now
been outmoded would seem to bear out the suggestion that
the readers of the epistle were laying too much stress upon
them, and were more unwilling than most Christian circles
to admit that these features of Judaism belonged to the
dead past.

VIII

THE TRUE TABERNACLE
8.1-5

We now come to the longest consistently theological section of the epistle which carries us on to 10.18. This is also as the Author tells us (v. 1) the crown of his argument. So far he has maintained that Christ, who is the human expression of the mind and purpose of God, is also the true High Priest, superseding all holders of that office in the old dispensation. Now he is to show the nature of the sacrifice offered by Christ, the place of offering and what the sacrifice achieves. He urges his readers to think of the heavenly sanctuary where the TRUE High Priest now intercedes for men. The distinction is between the earthly Holy Place in the Temple at Jerusalem, which was modelled on the Tabernacle of the Exodus, and its heavenly archetype which is the TRUE TABERNACLE. This idea goes back to the instructions given to Moses at Sinai to build a sanctuary where God might meet with his people (Ex. 25.9-40: Num. 8.4). His orders were to model the Tabernacle on the 'pattern' which God laid down. Thus arose the view that the Holy Place in the Temple, which was the successor of the Tabernacle, was the earthly and visible copy of an invisible sanctuary in heaven. In the intertestamental period, which was a breeding ground for speculation of this kind, it was maintained that the heavenly Tabernacle was not only equipped with the divinely designed furnishings of which the Temple contained the replicas, but that in it ministering angels offered atonement and intercessions for the sins of men.

THE HEAVENLY PATTERN

This distinction, as may well be imagined, found strong

support in such Jewish minds as had come under the influence of Greek philosophy. The Alexandian school, under the guidance of Philo, were familiar with the attempt to harmonize the Old Testament with Plato. Such a contrast as that between heavenly 'patterns' and earthly counterparts corresponded to the Platonic contrast between earthly shadow and heavenly substance. While this concept undoubtedly played a part in the Author's approach to the question, it would not be correct to say that it dominated his thought here or elsewhere in the Epistle. With him speculation is always subservient to theology. His main concern is with the heavenly Priesthood of Jesus, his intercession with God for men, and only secondarily does he think of this as the reality of which the man-made ordinances of the Temple are the reflection. It is rather a distinction between what is perfect and what is imperfect, man's fallible attempts to get right with God compared with God's perfect provision of an at-one-ment. When the Author says that if Jesus were on earth there would be no room for him to exercise his priesthood, since there is already the levitical order in operation, he is of course not implying that such a priesthood is adequate. Christians who are already living in touch with the unseen world cannot be content with anything less than the ministry of the Priest who serves there.

THE BETTER COVENANT
8.6-13

This heavenly ministry of Christ is of a higher order than any earthly ministry because he is the means of bringing about a BETTER COVENANT which rests upon BETTER PROMISES.

We have already had a reference to the New Covenant which came into being through Jesus (7.22). Now the subject is dealt with at greater length. The New Covenant

is better than the Old because the PROMISES contained in
God's words to Jeremiah are more far reaching than his
promises to Moses at the institution of the Old Covenant.
The Author then quotes in full the notable passage from
Jer. 31.31-34 which deals with this.

THE OLD COVENANT

When the Hebrews came as a nomadic tribe from the
Arabian desert into the Fertile Crescent and pastured their
flocks on the hillsides of Palestine, their religious beliefs
would seem to have been little different from those of their
neighbours. The radical break came at the Exodus when
under the guidance of Moses and as a result of their
astounding deliverance from slavery in Egypt they pledged
themselves to the God who had rescued them. They had
been plucked from a living death and set on the road to
new life: chosen for some purpose that they only gradually
came to see. Through no merit of their own, but by the
loving-kindness of God, they had been singled out and
placed in a relationship to God that no other people of the
ancient world shared. The word they used for this relationship was 'covenant'. It was a partnership between God on
the one hand, whom they pledged themselves to serve, and a
people who would receive his favour and protection in so
far as they maintained their obedience to him. The terms
of this obedience were the Ten Commandments and the
Law that derived from them. From the Exodus onwards
and from the moment of commitment at Sinai (Ex. 24) Israel
was the People of the Covenant. Their long and chequered
subsequent history may be summed up as a perpetual failure
to keep their side of the bargain despite the exhortation and
example of the minority within the nation who strove to
maintain the high standards that Moses had set them.

THE BETTER PROMISE

In the end, as prophet after prophet had foretold, the

nation came to grief, and the Judgement of God descended
upon the People who had betrayed his trust. The Holy City
was captured and destroyed and the best of the nation was
carried off into exile. The Covenant had apparently come
to an end. Yet there were some among the prophets who
refused to believe that God had spoken his last word, and
who trusted that somehow or other the love of God would
prove stronger than the evil of men. It was in this conviction that Jeremiah, about the time of the fall of Jerusalem
in 586 B.C. wrote the words which the Author quotes.
Although the House of Israel was scattered like a house of
cards, Jeremiah was given the insight that a New Covenant
would take the place of the Old. It would not be written
on tablets of stone as had been the case at Sinai, nor would
it depend on the holy soil of Canaan or the sacred walls of
the Temple. It would be a new relationship which would
make possible what the Old Covenant had failed to do.
Israel would be God's people and he would be their God
because he would forgive their sins, thus making it possible
for every man to approach him, to know him, and to do
his will. That this personal relationship to God by which he
would remove all barriers between himself and his people
would be realized with the coming of God's Messiah is
indicated by the prophet's use of the technical Messianic
phrase AFTER THOSE DAYS.

THE NEW COVENANT

It was the conviction of the early Church, based on our
Lord's own words (Luke 22.20), that the New Covenant had
come into being through him, and that the New Israel, the
reconstituted People of God, had inherited this 'better
promise' and all that it involved. The Author shares this
certainty, adding (v. 13) that even in Jeremiah's day the
fact that he spoke of a New Covenant indicated that the old
one was already as good as dead. He will now go on to
show that the real weakness of the Old Covenant was that

IX

THE TABERNACLE
9.1-5

THE AUTHOR AND JEREMIAH

The Author now embarks on a description of the furnishings
and ritual of the Tabernacle which may seem at times to
take us into regions which have only the remotest connection
with the Christian life to-day. Let us therefore not fail to
see the point which the Author is striving to make and which
connects closely with Jeremiah's words. The essence of the
Covenant relationship was that there should exist between
God and his people a bond of fellowship based on love and
service. Worship and obedience on the part of man, grace
and mercy on the part of God should be the marks of such
true communion. What the Author is saying here is that
communion with God was prevented under the old dispensation, and he sees the arrangements of the Tabernacle as
symbolizing the breakdown of the Covenant relationship on
man's side. God in his mercy has however provided a way
out of this impasse through Christ, making it now possible
for men to render him the worship and obedience which are
his due. Thus although it may seem, and indeed is doubtless the case, that in heralding a New Covenant Jeremiah
was not primarily thinking of the ritual aspect of the relationship between God and man, he had intrinsically the same
end in view as the Author, namely the establishment of a
right relationship with God.

THE NATIONAL SHRINE

In order to lead up to the proof of his contention that
Jesus had made the perfect sacrifice once for all (7.27) which

bridged the gulf between man and God and made true communion possible, the Author has to paint the picture of how men had previously tried in vain to achieve this through the cultus of the Old Covenant. We are given a description of the heart of Temple worship which centred on the national shrine, the Tabernacle. No words can describe the sanctity of this place in the eyes of the Jews. The Psalms reflect the passionate devotion with which the worship of the Temple was regarded. Its music and pageantry, its ritual and colour must have made its services memorable. To take part in one of the sacred processions up the steep hill and through the gates of Jerusalem to the Holy Place on Mount Zion was for the Jews who came there on pilgrimage from Palestine or overseas the nearest approach to the Presence of God.

The vast Temple area with its series of courts strictly allocated to the various classes of worshippers had at its centre the Tabernacle, the successor of the Tent of the Exodus (Ex. 33.7), and open only to the priesthood. It was entered through a thick screen and was divided into an outer and inner sanctuary. The larger of the two, which was twice the size of the smaller, was known as the Holy Place, and the smaller as the Holy of Holies. In the Author's description of the furnishings of these chapels we are given a composite picture. From various minor inaccuracies it may be gathered that the Author had never set foot in the Temple himself. His knowledge is based on the biblical description in Ex. 25f. with additional features which according to tradition had been associated with the sanctuary.

A COMPOSITE PICTURE

The narrative in Ex. 25f. is supplied by the Priestly editors of the Pentateuch, who presumably give there an ideal reconstruction of what was supposed to have been the divine pattern communicated to Moses. In actual fact there were three Temples. The first was that of Solomon, built in the

tenth century B.C., which was destroyed in 586 B.C. when
Nebuchadnezzar of Babylon captured Jerusalem. The second
was the post-exilic building of Zerubbabel (*ca.* 520 B.C.),
and the third was Herod's grandiose edifice dating from just
before the beginning of the Christian era. This was the
Temple which existed in the Author's day, but it is difficult
to say from his description of its furnishings which particular
stage in its history is being referred to. The Ark of the
Covenant, for example, seems to have disappeared after
586 B.C., and before that time it was supposed to hold nothing but the stone tablets of the Ten Commandments. In
the second and third Temples the Holy of Holies would
appear to have been completely empty. The Author is, however, only concerned to give a piece of background for his
theology and not an archaeological excursus or a contemporary catalogue. The general impression he gives more
or less fits such facts as we possess.

THE CANDLESTICK

The Tent of the Exodus had in the course of time developed, as we have seen, into a chapel with two compart-
ments separated from each other by a heavy ornamental
curtain or VEIL. In the outer section or Holy Place was a
lampstand. This was the seven-branched CANDLESTICK,
which was carried off by Titus as part of the spoils of war
when Jerusalem was finally sacked by the Romans in A.D. 70.
It is still to be seen in bas-relief on the Arch of Titus in
the Forum in Rome, recalling the triumphal procession of
the victor. Its original purpose had been to provide light
in the windowless antechamber, but it had come to sym-
bolize the uninterrupted worship of God that was offered
there.

THE TABLE OF THE BREAD

The second feature was the TABLE OF THE BREAD. In
earlier times this was no doubt regarded as nourishment for

Yahweh as was the smoke of burnt offerings. It had come
to signify however a thankoffering of the fruits of the earth
which God provided for the needs of the people. Wine was
included in the thankoffering, which was changed at weekly
intervals.

THE ALTAR OF INCENSE

The Author describes this as being beyond the VEIL in the
Holy of Holies. It is very doubtful if this was ever the case,
since it had to be tended daily by the ordinary priests who
were not allowed to pass through the curtain. The reason
for the confusion is that in the Septuagint translation of
Ex. 30.1-10 which describes the ALTAR OF INCENSE, the
Greek word may mean either ' just in front of ' or ' beside '
the veil. In the original Hebrew it is quite clear that this
altar stood in the outer compartment. At one time there
had only been the great altar in the open air for burning
the fat of the sacrificial animals, which was considered to
be Yahweh's portion. Later there had been added this inner
altar on which nothing was burned except spices which
provided incense, and symbolized the perpetual offering of
sacrifices. Ex. 30.1-10 is in fact an addendum of a later
date to the sacrificial arrangements described in the previous
chapters.

THE ARK OF THE COVENANT

Beyond the inner curtain, known as the Veil, was the
Holy of Holies. This contained the Ark of the Covenant,
originally probably a plain portable and smallish wooden
box dating from the Exodus, which held the stone tablets
of the Decalogue. It was thought in more primitive times to
be the dwelling place of Yahweh, who accompanied his
people into battle and won their victories. Its loss was
regarded as a national disaster (I Sam. 4). When it was
installed in the Temple, it was encased in gold and, according to the Author, held in addition to the Tablets of the

Decalogue, a POT OF MANNA and AARON'S ROD. This con-
flicts with the evidence of II Chron. 5.10, according to which
the Ark contained nothing but the two engraved Covenant
Tablets. The pot of manna may at some later point have
been added as a reminder of God's provision of food for
the people during the Exodus, in accordance with the injunction of Ex. 16.32-34. Similarly Aaron's rod, which was the
symbolic guarantee of the levitical succession (Num.
17.1-11), would appropriately have found an honoured place
in this chief ornament of the Tabernacle. On the other hand
the Author may have got his facts wrong, since in both cases
the injunction to Moses is to lay them up not in the Ark
but in front of it. Rabbinic tradition however maintained
that these sacred objects had later been placed within the
ancient palladium of the Hebrews.

THE MERCY-SEAT

Most holy of all was the MERCY-SEAT, the symbol of the
Throne of God. This suggestive name was Tyndale's translation of Luther's rendering of the Hebrew word which
originally meant a 'lid'. But from the thought of Yahweh's
presence in the Ark, which must therefore be kept shut,
came the idea that the nearest approach to him was the
covering. This slab of pure gold, because of the rites that
came to be associated with it, was called in Greek the
'place of propitiation'. Normally the great altar outside
was regarded as the place of propitiation, but on the Day
of Atonement the Mercy-seat was splashed with blood with
this end in view. Above the Mercy-seat spread the wings
of the CHERUBIM, strange composite sphinx-like figures, half-
man half-animal, doubtless derived from Babylonian, Egyptian and Canaanite mythology. They were guardians of the
Throne of the invisible God.

THE FAILURE OF THE RITUAL
9.6-10

The Author has outlined the furnishings of the Tabernacle, adding that he cannot do more than mention them as incidental to his main purpose. For he has now to deal with the ritual itself. In and out of the main part of the Tabernacle goes a daily stream of priests; tending the Lamp, renewing the Incense, and every seven days changing the Bread. But into the place of the Presence of God only once each year goes one man, a sinful mortal called to the office of HIGH PRIEST, bearing in his hands the blood of animals, in the hope of cleansing his own sins and the sins of the people he represents, but even then only the sins of ignorance. The Author implies that despite the richness of the furnishings of the sanctuary and the meticulous performance of an elaborate cultus the end result is negligible. The mountain labours and produces a mouse. The ritual of the Outer Tabernacle is useless, a daily rigmarole accomplishing nothing. The offices of the Inner Tabernacle are little better, since they cover only the sins that men are unaware of having committed.

SINS OF CONSCIENCE

This even in Old Testament times was recognized by the prophets who, speaking in the power of the HOLY SPIRIT, condemned the empty ceremonial of the Temple and proclaimed its inadequacy to enable men to enter the true HOLY PLACE, and approach the Throne of God in heaven (v. 8). So long as the ritual of the outer sanctuary receives the importance that has been attached to it, and so long as only the High Priest may enter the inner sanctuary, the way to God is barred for ordinary men. All of which, continues the Author (v. 9), is symbolic of the present age. The Outer Tabernacle is still represented by Judaism with its meaningless sacrificial system, preventing all but one sinful man

once a year from entering the Presence of God. The fundamental weakness of the whole cultus is that it cannot deal
with the sins of CONSCIENCE, the sense of guilt that comes
from moral failure, which is the real barrier that keeps
men from God. The ritual is concerned with trivial con-
traventions of the laws dealing with eating and drinking
forbidden things at forbidden times, and with failure to
comply with rules about ceremonial ablutions. The sacrificial system being a material thing itself could only deal
with material sins of this kind. But now that the New Age
has dawned, the TIME OF REFORMATION, the whole apparatus
of the Tabernacle has been superseded. The Outer Tabernacle and what it represents has become archaic and the
Inner Tabernacle has been supplanted, since by the forgiveness of sins the way to the true Presence of God in heaven,
and not merely the earthly symbol, has been thrown open
to all who will follow Christ there.

MEATS AND DRINKS

It may be noted here that those scholars who consider this
letter to have been written not specifically to Jewish Christians or, if to Jewish Christians, then to some who were
toying with the same type of Gnostic speculation as the
Colossians, suggest that the reference in v. 10 to MEATS AND
DRINKS refers to ascetic tendencies. They would say that
the Author is trying to show that Christianity does not con-
sist in treating the material things of life, like the needs of
the body, as unworthy of those who have been enlightened
by Christian truth. It surely seems much more probable
that the readers were in effect ultra-Jewish in their approach
to the Gospel, that they tended to lay stress on such things
as the dietary regulations on which they had been brought
up, and that they questioned the unrestricted freedom in these
matters which the development of the Church was encourag-
ing. Doubtless they felt that in throwing overboard the
traditions of the past they were sacrificing part of their birth-

right, which had after all for centuries been regarded as the proper obedience of the same God whom as Christians they now worshipped.

It is perhaps not without significance that in writing to the Church at Rome St. Paul complains that it was unduly preoccupied with this question of ceremonially clean or unclean food (Rom. 14). It should not surprise us that this played so large a role either in the Jewish Church or the Christian Church. There was no more obvious way, apart from observing the Sabbath, of impressing on themselves and their pagan neighbours that their religion meant something to them, that it was not a matter of following their own inclinations but that they recognized certain clear-cut obligations to God. It was of course a much easier way of satisfying the conscience than by facing the complex decisions and moral ambiguities of a life lived under the Gospel.

A MODERN PARALLEL

The modern equivalent of the Jewish food regulations which the readers apparently cherished so fondly might perhaps be represented in the Christian Church by the advocates of Prohibition, Sabbath Observance, and Anti-Gambling. The general body of Church opinion while favouring moderation in drinking, enjoining respect for Sunday, and deploring the growth of betting does not see the answer to these problems to be a simple one, and would not wish to identify Christian witness with clamorous advocacy of what are in effect side issues.

THE TRUE SACRIFICE
9.11-14

But now Christ, continues the Author, has come as High Priest, not of a fallible human attempt to obtain salvation, but of true salvation. There is an interesting variant in the

MSS. at this point. Whereas the majority of MSS. read THE
GOOD THINGS TO COME, i.e. the full realization of perfect communion with God, which is only possible beyond this world
as we know it, a few MSS. have the more unusual, and
therefore more probably original reading, THE GOOD THINGS
THAT ARE COME. It is the difference between saying that the
perfect relationship with God, which is the aim of the
Christian life, is wholly an other-worldly experience, and
claiming that to some extent at least we are able to enter
into that relationship here and now.

OUTWARD AND INWARD CLEANSING

Christ then has entered the heavenly shrine which is no
man-made structure but the PATTERN (8.5) or original of the
imperfect earthly Tabernacle. He has entered the Presence
of God not by means of the BLOOD OF GOATS AND CALVES,
by sprinkling which on the Mercy-seat the human High
Priests thought to atone for the sins of themselves and the
people (Lev. 16). No, he has entered THROUGH HIS OWN
BLOOD, the symbol of his life. The Son of God has given
himself as the perfect means of making men at one with
God. This he has not done as an annual event but ONCE
FOR ALL, and has thereby liberated from sin not merely a
nation for a year but all men for ever.

We have already seen the purpose of the BLOOD OF GOATS
AND BULLS. The Author now adds the ASHES OF A HEIFER,
which were mixed with water and sprinkled on anyone who
had according to the Law been ceremonially defiled by
touching a corpse (Num. 19.9f.). It almost looks as if he
added this as the acme of futility. All of these might make
men's bodies ritually clean, but what could they do for their
consciences? Only the blood of Christ, whose sinlessness
made him as free of moral blemish as the cattle were out-
wardly UNBLEMISHED, could cleanse the inward impurity of
conscience.

THE CLEANSING POWER OF BLOOD

The Author has inherited as a fact not to be questioned and not requiring proof that blood cleanses. It was a principle embedded in the sacred Law and derived from much more ancient practice. The basic idea is always reconciliation, the restoration of the right relationship with the deity. However primitive the religious beliefs may be, the whole conception of sacrifice is that of effecting at-one-ment. In this particular case the conception of the cleansing power of blood probably goes back to a superstitious belief that the blood of an animal consecrated at the altar derives supernatural power from its contact with the deity, and that this in turn is by the rite of sprinkling communicated to the worshipper, who is thereby cleansed from whatever has placed a barrier between himself and the god.

It should be emphasized that nowhere in this Hebrew theory of sacrifice is there any forensic element. There is no question of the victim paying the penalty that the worshipper should pay. When the Author, therefore, sublimates the idea of sacrifice and speaks of the blood of Christ cleansing the conscience, it is in the characteristically Old Testament sense of forgiveness and reconciliation. His thought is that the eternal sinless Spirit of Christ, through the offering of it to God, works on the spirit of man, purifying it and enabling it, through contact with him, to enter into full communion with God.

THE PURPOSE OF CHRIST'S SACRIFICE

In the language of the epistle, therefore, Christ is both Priest and Victim. The Cross was an act in time, but since Christ is eternal his offering of himself has eternal validity. It cleanses men from DEAD WORKS (i.e. sin) not merely from dead bodies, because it is the life blood of Christ the Son of God and not of animals. He offered himself voluntarily, not like the helpless beasts dragged to the altar. Unlike

theirs his offering was of a life not extinguishable by death
(i.e. THROUGH ETERNAL SPIRIT) and WITHOUT (MORAL) BLEM-
ISH. In all respects, therefore, the self-sacrifice of Christ was
superior to the sacrificial system of the Old Covenant. Its
whole purpose was to enable men to SERVE (i.e. to worship)
THE LIVING GOD. This then is the climax to which the
Author's argument has been rising. What Christ did by
offering himself was to make possible the true worship of
God by bridging the gulf that men's sins had created and
restoring the right relationship between God and man.

CHRIST THE MEDIATOR
9.15-22

Before trying to understand the thought of this next
section we must first note that in the course of it the Author
uses the same Greek word in two different senses, as the
marginal note in the R.V. recognizes. In v. 15 the word
is used to mean a 'covenant', and in vv. 16 and 17 it
means a 'will'. The point is not very important, but it will
avoid confusion if we realize that he is using the same word
in different ways.

FOR OLD AND NEW ISRAEL

A New Covenant was necessary because the old covenant-
relationship was unable to bring about the perfect fellowship,
or INHERITANCE, which was PROMISED by God to his people.
But since the prelude to that new relationship had to be a
complete cleansing of the accumulated guilt of the past, and
since there can be no forgiveness without sacrifice, the death
of Christ was necessary. As in the case of a will, people
can only inherit what they have been promised if death has
taken place. Christ's death achieves the forgiveness
(REDEMPTION) of all the past sins of the People of God. That
is to say, the People of God, THEY THAT HAVE BEEN CALLED,

who, until Christ came, were unable to have a perfect relationship with God because the means of forgiveness were inadequate, are now able to do so.

Notice that the Author makes no radical distinction between the People of God of the Old and New Covenants. They are all the People of the promised inheritance, from Abraham onwards. The roll of honour which appears in chapters 11-12 includes the saints of Old Israel as well as of New Israel. The Old Israel did not in fact receive the PROMISE in their own day because Christ had not yet come to make it possible. It seems that the Author regards Christ's death as retrospectively effective in opening the way to God for all, whether in Old or New Israel, who have been called, and, of course, who have responded with REPENTANCE.

THE FIRST COVENANT

He goes on now to speak of the FIRST COVENANT. This was the pact between God and Israel at Sinai, as described in Exodus 24. The Author is quoting from memory since there is no reference in that account to GOATS, WATER, SCARLET WOOL or HYSSOP. Water was used to dilute blood, and hyssop twigs bound with scarlet thread were used as a sprinkler in ceremonial decontamination (e.g. Num. 19.6; Lev. 14.6; Ex. 12.22). Nor does Moses sprinkle the BOOK of the Covenant with blood, but only the altar and the people. Likewise the TABERNACLE and its VESSELS, when they came into existence later, and not at this point, were cleansed with oil and not with blood (Ex. 40.9-10). The Author's enthusiasm for his argument carries him too far. It is of more interest however to notice how, instinctively, he changes the words of Ex. 24.8: BEHOLD THE BLOOD OF THE COVENANT, to: THIS IS THE BLOOD OF THE COVENANT, doubtless a reminiscence of the words used by Jesus at the Last Supper (Mark 14.24).

THE ESSENCE OF THE COVENANT RELATIONSHIP

His conclusion is that according to the Law the restoration of the proper relationship to God was with few exceptions (e.g. Lev. 5.11-13) only accomplished by the shedding of blood. That is to say, that even under the imperfect Old Covenant, and however little at-one-ment was effected, blood had to be shed. Basically the Author's argument is sound. The Covenant relationship was fundamental to the life of Israel, and the whole point of the Law was to keep that relationship intact. It was the recognition that an individual by sinning could put himself outside the Covenant, as well as contaminate the whole community and bring God's judgement upon it, that made individual acts of atonement necessary, just as it was the recognition that the whole nation by its sins of ignorance and omission could put itself outside the Covenant that led to the institution of a National Day of Atonement. The author is therefore entitled to quote in a general way different sections of the Law and relate them to the institution of the Covenant.

THE MEDIATOR

The point to which the Author is leading us becomes clear when we consider the two apparently widely differing forms of the first Covenant in the Old Testament. That Covenant had two stages. There was the Covenant between Yahweh and Abraham (Gen. 15) by which the Hebrews were selected as the nucleus of the People of God. There was also the Covenant between Yahweh and Israel (Ex. 24.4-8) to which the Author directly refers, by which the religious significance of the Covenant relationship was intensified. In the Genesis narrative Yahweh in the form of fire, and presumably Abraham as well, are represented as passing between the divided carcasses of animals, thus, as it were, becoming one by means of a third party. The life of the animal, believed to reside in its blood, was set free by its death to provide

G

the uniting factor, and each party was supposed to enter into the life of the animal by passing between its halved body.

In the Exodus story Yahweh is represented by the altar. The blood of the sacrificial animals is then sprinkled on the altar and on the people. Once more Yahweh and his people are united in a pact and the liberated life-blood of the animals makes them one. When therefore all types of sacrifice in the levitical regulations involve the sprinkling of blood, the point behind them is to reflect the significance of the Covenant rite and to subserve the Covenant relationship. The function of the Covenant animal in all Jewish ritual was therefore essentially mediatory, and it is as MEDIATOR in this sense that the Author regards Jesus. The shedding of his blood was no transaction to appease an angry God or to buy off the Devil. His surrendered life was the means of uniting God and man and thereby restoring the proper relationship. Only one who was both Son of God and Son of Man could do this.

THE FINALITY OF THE SACRIFICE
OF CHRIST
9.23-28

THE CLEANSING OF HEAVEN

The Author returns to his earlier picture of the heavenly pattern of the Sanctuary and its earthly copy. The Day of Atonement regulations prescribed sacrificial ritual, as we have seen, for cleansing the sins of High Priest and people. But the blood of the animals was also regarded as cleansing the Tabernacle itself and the altar from the taint of sin, as if the presence of sinful priests and the practice of imperfect sacrifices had over the year left behind a stain that must be washed away. It is in this figurative sense that the Author speaks of Christ having cleansed the HEAVENLY THINGS with his sacrifice. Perhaps he thought of the dark cloud of the sins of mankind casting so deep a shadow and so obscuring the light of God's glory that nothing could sweep it from the heavens but the atoning work of the Son. At all events the metaphor is of the same order as that of Christ's entrance through the VEIL. Both represent his opening up of the way to God.

THE FINAL VICTORY

Now the Author contrasts again the sacrifice of Christ with the levitical sacrifices (cf. vv. 11-12); the High Priest entering the local sanctuary of Jerusalem with his annual offering of an impersonal sacrifice, Jesus entering the very Presence of God in heaven offering himself to God once for all. If his atonement had not been a final act of God, so great has been the mass of mankind's sin from the beginning of time that he would have had to make atonement not once but many times. This, however, is the first and last. No time remains for Christ to be incarnated and to die again, for the end of the present order as men know it is at hand. His sacrifice is therefore the climax of the AGES. Even in the case of an ordinary man death is final, and nothing remains but the Judgement of God. In the case of Christ nothing is left now but the Final Victory to complete the work of SALVATION. The reference to the Second Advent, in which the Author uses the conventional symbol of a reappearance of Christ, may be suggested by the reappearance of the High Priest from the Holy of Holies on the Day of Atonement. This was the sign that the atonement had been completed. So the Second Coming of Christ will be the final proof of the efficacy of his sacrifice. Sin having now been finally removed, when he returns there will be no barrier to keep men from God and they will become his for ever.

TO BEAR THE SINS OF MANY: cf. Isa. 53.11-12: Mark 10.45. Neither here nor elsewhere does the use of MANY imply that some are omitted. The point in each reference is to stress the scope of the sacrifice, 'many' as distinct from 'few'.

The Author shares the expectation of the early Church that the final end of the Old Age and the full implementation of the New Age which has already begun will be marked by the Triumph of Christ. He makes little use of the apocalyptic mythology which suggests a personal physical return of Jesus to earth. His main emphasis is on Christ having entered the eternal sanctuary where he makes an eternal intercession with the Father for men. Such a conception makes hardly less use of symbolic language than does the conventional jargon of the apocalyptists, but it is less open to imaginative embellishment. It suggests rather than attempts to describe an order of existence which is beyond our comprehension. The Author's reference here is probably not a concession to popular early Church apocalypticism but, as has been suggested, an allusion to the Day of Atonement. In principle, however, it is fully in keeping with his repeated emphasis on the Church's Hope.

X

THE FINAL VERDICT ON
ANIMAL SACRIFICE
10.1-4

In the first eighteen verses of this chapter the Author gathers
together what he has been saying about the significance of
the death of Christ and brings to an end the theological
section which began at 8.1. He comes back first of all to
the failure of the ritual sacrifices of the Temple, which he
sums up as THE LAW. This, as we have seen, is not what
St. Paul would have meant by the Law, but both interpreta-
tions are legitimate, since the Law was equally concerned
with moral behaviour, which was the Apostle's primary concern, and ritual practice, which is of paramount interest to
the Author. Both aspects were designed to establish the
right relationship to God.

SHADOW AND IMAGE

But this, says the Author, thinking of the ceremonial of
the Temple, is precisely what the Law was unable to do.
Falling back again, perhaps unconsciously, on the Platonic
shadow-substance theory, he speaks of the Law as the
SHADOW of the true IMAGE. In this case it is the difference
between the Old Covenant and the New that is meant. There
are in fact three stages involved in the Author's thought.
The Law was the SHADOW OF THE GOOD THINGS TO COME,
i.e. a dim reflection of that perfect knowledge of God and
fellowship with him which the New Covenant promised.
Both of these were conditional on the removal of the barrier
which sin erected between man and God. With the coming
of Christ and especially since his death, which inaugurated

the New Covenant, his people could enjoy the IMAGE OF THE GOOD THINGS TO COME, i.e. a foretaste of that complete communion which was their promised inheritance. The ultimate state when the People of God would live in un-interrupted sonship to God, the full realization of THE GOOD THINGS TO COME, lies however in a state of being beyond that which we know.

REMEMBRANCE IS SOMETHING—

Nothing of this could be achieved by the incessant repeti-tion of animal sacrifice. If the ritual had been an adequate means of drawing near to God surely there would have been no need to repeat it time after time. The reason why it went on year after year was simply that men knew within themselves that their CONSCIENCE was still burdened by the accumulated guilt of the past. They were still separated from God. Indeed the ritual did no more than bring men's sins to their minds. St. Paul had said the same thing in Rom. 3.20. The word used for REMEMBRANCE is that which is used in the words of the Institution of Holy Communion (I Cor. 11.24): THIS DO IN REMEMBRANCE OF ME. It means more than casually recalling to memory, and suggests rather making vividly and consciously present again.

—BUT NOT ENOUGH

Yet the Author would no doubt have added that even a REMEMBRANCE was better than nothing. That men should even once a year on the Day of Atonement be brought to a recognition of the gulf that existed between the holiness of God and their own sorry performance was not without value. Therefore the Law was at least a SHADOW, a reflection of reality, more than a hint of the truth. But at best it was transitory, earth-bound and imperfect compared with the image of the eternal heavenly reality. Men must be certain that they are forgiven not merely for the time being but for ever. Otherwise the burden of guilt remains. But eternal forgiveness, concludes the Author trenchantly, cannot come through THE BLOOD OF BULLS AND GOATS. That is IMPOSSIBLE.

THE OFFERING OF THE BODY
OF CHRIST
10.5-10

PSALM 40 IN HEBREW AND GREEK

This passage is in some ways the most profound moment in the Author's conception of the High Priesthood of Jesus. Before grappling with it let us look first at the Psalm which he quotes and which he uses as proof of his point. The fortieth Psalm is one of thanksgiving for deliverance from danger. In the course of it the writer (vv. 6-8) speaks of his realization that what God demands is the obedience of a willing response to his loving-kindness. God's Law has become part of his inmost self. To do his bidding is his delight. He has seen that the true service of God is not in the fulfilment of the ritual sacrifices of the Temple, but in a faithful and grateful heart. It is a noble and beautiful expression of a constantly reiterated theme of the prophets.

The Hebrew version as reproduced in the Old Testament has however a striking variation from the quotation given by the Author, who naturally uses the Greek translation on which he had been brought up. At some point in the early MSS. of the Septuagint an important scribal error must have occurred, for what was originally in the Hebrew MINE EARS HAST THOU OPENED has become in the Greek A BODY HAST THOU PREPARED FOR ME. A comparison of the phrase in the two languages shows how this could easily have happened. It does, however, alter the sense considerably, and as can be seen from the epistle, allows the Author to use it as a prediction of the Incarnation and the supersession of the Law by Christ.

THE TRANSMISSION OF SCRIPTURE

It is important to ask ourselves what this involves. Is it a misuse of Scripture and does it render the Author's argument fallacious? It could only do so if we regard the text of Scripture, as the Author regarded it, as preserved from all human fallibility and inspired by the Holy Spirit. We recognize more clearly now that not only is the Word of God transmitted to us through the minds of men who see part of its truth and not all of it, but also that it is exposed to the same dangers of transmission as any other ancient writings. Translators' misunderstandings and copyists' errors are as likely to occur in Holy Scripture as elsewhere. We do not expect infallibility of thought or text in the Old Testament or its translations any more than we expect it in the New Testament, including the Epistle to the Hebrews.

THE OLD TESTAMENT IN THE EARLY CHURCH

On the other hand, as has been evident on more than one occasion, the Author, like the early Christians in general, was wiser than some modern devotees of the Scriptures in that he does not feel himself slavishly bound to a literal interpretation of the Old Testament. The early Church based its theology not on the Old Testament but on the historical ministry of Jesus. They searched the Scriptures, and if they found passages in the Old Testament that illuminated their understanding of what had happened they accepted them gladly. They neither tried to pour their theology into an Old Testament mould nor did they scruple to disregard apparently obvious parallels which they found unsuitable or to use Old Testament scriptures in a sense other than the original writer intended.

THE AUTHOR'S USE OF PSALM 40

Our Author would not have been in the least disturbed— nor would any New Testament writer—if he had been told

that there was a discrepancy between the original translation
and the Greek version which he was using, any more than
he would have been more than momentarily disturbed to be
told that David had not written the Psalms (cf. 4.7). The
conviction of the first Christians was that the New Age had
dawned and that they were living in a new dimension where
the Spirit of Christ had made all things new. In a general
way the Old Testament scriptures pointed to his coming
and expressed the hopes and prayers that had now been
fulfilled. Nevertheless their faith rested on no literalist
belief in the fulfilment of every isolated prediction of prophet
or psalmist but on the living power of the Risen Christ who
was constantly leading them into wider apprehension of the
truth of God than the Old Testament writers had ever dreamt
of.

In this passage from Ps. 40 therefore it does not invalidate
the Author's argument one whit that he attributes to the
Psalmist an idea which the Psalmist did not entertain,
because the Author's theological conclusions do not rest
upon what he believed the Psalmist to be saying but upon the
implications of the SALVATION SPOKEN THROUGH THE LORD
(2.3). The Old Testament text is in one sense a convenient
peg on which to hang his thoughts. His basic theme is
that Christ has superseded the Law, and he uses what, so
far as he knew, the Psalmist had said as further light on an
already established conclusion. Our concern is therefore not
with what the Psalmist said but with what was in the mind of
the Author.

THE ONLY ADEQUATE SACRIFICE

He regards the words as having been spoken by Christ to
God before his Incarnation. Addressing the Father he
speaks of his work on earth, culminating in his sacrificial
death, as his response to the will of God that he should by
his Incarnation and Death, which were foretold in the Scriptures, replace a sacrificial system which was unacceptable to

God. The Author's point is that the coming of Christ was in the purpose of God intended to supersede the unsatisfactory attempt of the Jewish cultus to establish the right relationship between himself and man. The sacrificial system was not wrong but it was inadequate. It has now been replaced by Christ's sacrifice of himself. God has superseded the FIRST in order that his will might be done by the SECOND.

By totally identifying himself with man, THROUGH THE OFFERING OF THE BODY, the Son of God has taken man's sin upon himself once and for all. In fact the practice of confessing the sins of men over the scapegoat and banishing it to the desert was useless. Guilt cannot be transferred from the sinner to an involuntary substitute, least of all a helpless animal. But in principle the practice was justified in that it recognized the need for a mediator. When such a Mediator as Christ, who came from God and went to God, appeared on earth, voluntarily took upon himself the whole range of human temptation and suffering, and was obedient to the will of God even to giving himself over to death for mankind, the true meaning behind the practice of animal sacrifice and the Day of Atonement became apparent. Christ put himself in man's place and bore his sin. By doing for men what they were unable to do for themselves, and what High Priests and scapegoats were unable to do for them, he lifted from their shoulders for ever the burden of accumulated sin, eased their guilty consciences, and enabled them to be at one with God. The slate was wiped clean and humanity was given a fresh start.

7. in the roll of the book

Before the present page system of bookbinding, sheets of parchment or papyrus were gummed together at the edges to form a continuous length. St. Matthew's Gospel for example extended to about thirty feet. This was then affixed at each end to a stick resembling a rolling pin, and a book was read by winding up one end with one hand and unwinding the other end with the other. The word ROLL comes from the knob of the stick round which the papyrus was wound. The Jewish Law is still read in synagogues from such rolls. Here the phrase means: 'It is written of me in the Law,' i.e. the Law, especially in its ritual sections dealing with sacrifice, pointed forward to Christ.

10. sanctified

The Author's use of the word here and in v. 14 is not Pauline. St. Paul uses the word 'justified' to mean what the Author intends to convey by 'sanctified', i.e. put into a right relationship with God. St. Paul uses 'sanctification' to indicate the process whereby a man once 'justified' grows up into the Christian life. This is the normal theological meaning.

THE EXALTED CHRIST
10.11-18

Finally the Author depicts the priests of the old regime, *standing*, trying busily and incessantly to do something to bring the worshippers into touch with God and achieving nothing, while Jesus *sits*, his work accomplished, at the right hand of God, now only awaiting his final triumph (cf. 1.13). With this magnificently imaginative picture, focusing the vain efforts of men to save themselves in the figure of the anxious and ineffective priest over against the serene majesty of the exalted Son of God enthroned in heaven, the Author has taken us in a few short verses through the whole gamut of the work of Christ: his pre-existence with God (v. 5), his incarnate life on earth (v. 10), his ascended and glorified life in heaven (v. 12), and his ultimate victory (v. 13). The unmistakable mark of the New Covenant as prophesied by Jeremiah (see 8.8f.) was to be the fulfilment of God's promise: THEIR SINS AND THEIR INIQUITIES WILL

I REMEMBER NO MORE. All that the Law had done was to
remind men of their sins (v. 3). What Jesus had done meant
that even God himself had forgotten their sins, had treated
them as though they had never been committed. In such a
case there could not possibly be any occasion for further
sacrifices. The need for them had disappeared for ever.
It almost looks as if the Author's readers not only wanted to
incorporate the Jewish dietary regulations into the Church,
but also felt that by forfeiting the Jewish sacrificial system,
and in particular the Day of Atonement, they had lost something precious. The Author's implicit reply, if this is so, is
that not only does an eternal Day of Atonement with a
heavenly High Priest, who has direct access to the true
Throne of Grace, secure for Christian people the only kind
of forgiveness of sins which is valid, but also that the proper
response of the Christian is to celebrate every day as a Day
of Atonement in humility and penitence. At all events it is
from the contemplation of these sublime mysteries that the
Author turns to their implications for the ordinary life of
ordinary people.

PILGRIMS' PROGRESS
10.19–13.25

In the course of the Author's theological argument, it may
have crossed our minds from time to time that not only
was there a certain remoteness from twentieth century life
in the parallel between the ceremonial of the Jewish Temple
and the life and death of Jesus, but also that the finality of
ONCE AND FOR ALL seemed to imply that what the self-
sacrifice of Jesus had accomplished left nothing for us to
do. If his dying for us means that he has taken our sins
upon himself, does that imply that we may henceforth sin
with impunity, or that without further effort on our part
the right relationship with God which Christ obtained for
us will be maintained?

Let us be quite clear about what has been said. Briefly it amounts to this. The Author's problem has been one of relationships. How can we become the kind of men and women God meant us to be, knowing, as we believe, that only in that way can we be said to be truly alive and to be experiencing all that life has to offer? The first step must be to know that this aim is not illusory, some will-o'-the-wisp fancy that ends in disaster and despair. If, for example, we have some sense of our own failure, our selfishness and our mixed motives; if we recognize that even when we do our best to live the good life, our best is a tattered caricature of what it ought to be, then our first reaction is bound to be one of frustration and disillusionment. There is no limit to the active or potential evil of which we know ourselves to be capable. The crimes of others we recognize to be latent within ourselves. Given the same chance to do wrong, which of us is not obliged to say: 'There but for the grace of God go I.'

More than that we feel that we are caught up in the accumulated evil of our society. We are part of history and we inherit the guilt of the civilization into which we are born. We share responsibility for its political, economic and social failures. We cannot escape from the moral ambiguities, the iniquities and tolerated evils of which even the most enlightened democracies are guilty. This is the human situation, humanity's perennial plight. Over against it all stands God, and even if we do not feel the shattering contrast between his Holiness and our sinful selves with the same intensity as did Isaiah (chapter 6.1f.), we must feel something of the utter helplessness and hopelessness of ever struggling out of this morass, to set our feet upon the path that leads to him.

This is the problem that the Author has been facing, and his answer has been that God stoops down to pull us out of the bog and places us on solid ground. He not only puts a signpost on the road that leads upward to himself, but gives us a Guide for our journey, who assures us of what awaits us at the top. Two things however we must do ourselves. We must hold out our hands to be rescued, and after reaching solid ground we must start at once to climb the path. In theological jargon the holding out of our hands to God is repentance; the recognition of our plight, from which only God can save us, coupled with a determination to keep our faces turned towards him. Similarly God's act of rescue is theologically speaking effected through the Incarnation of his Son. God comes down into our morass in Jesus Christ to lift us up to himself. Jesus sets us on solid ground and points the way to God. This is the Atonement. The road is steep, tangled with briers and treacherous in parts, but we know that Jesus has gone before us, and that he has cleared a path and cut footholds where we shall need them. But climb the road we must, because at the end of it is the fulfilment of our destiny. Theologians, apart from the Author (see 10.10), would call this Sanctification, and it is to this upward journey of the Christian that the Author now turns, but he will speak of it in his own way.

THROUGH THE VEIL
10.19-25

As a result of what Christ has done, says the Author, we may with confident assurance (BOLDNESS) approach God through him. When he speaks of THE NEW AND LIVING WAY to God which Jesus has inaugurated, he thinks of it no doubt as a LIVING way as opposed to the false way of reliance on dead animals, and, significantly enough, the Greek word he uses here for NEW meant originally 'newly-killed'. Further, we are reminded that our Lord spoke of himself as the WAY, THE TRUTH AND THE LIFE (John 14.6). The way has been opened and Jesus has gone on ahead.

Before his death the way was closed and a VEIL hung between us and God. This is of course an allusion to the veil or curtain in the Temple at Jerusalem which concealed the sacred mysteries of the Sanctuary from the worshippers in the Temple court. Behind it lay the symbols of God's Presence. In speaking of the veil as the FLESH of Jesus, the Author uses the same metaphor as St. Mark (15.38) when he describes the rending of the veil of the Temple at the Crucifixion. Both writers mean that by the death of Christ the way to God was opened. The Author compares the rending of the body of Christ in death to the tearing apart of the veil which until then concealed the HOLY PLACE. Not only have we a NEW WAY to God, but we have also a GREAT High PRIEST, who is ever present with God interceding for us.

Therefore let us approach him sincerely, and trustingly. Jesus has passed beyond the VEIL, but we know that he is there and that we have even now communion with God through him. That is what the Author means by FULNESS OF FAITH, and he will shortly have more to say of it with illustrations from past history. Our hearts have been SPRINKLED FROM AN EVIL CONSCIENCE. Here the allusion is probably to the ritual sprinkling of the priesthood with blood as a mark of cleaning from sin (Ex. 29.20-21). The Christian acknowledging the self-offering of Christ for his sake, feels the burden of guilt lifted from him. His heart has been sprinkled with the blood of Christ. Similarly as the priests' bodies were cleansed with PURE WATER (Ex. 29.4) so the Christian is inwardly cleansed by the outward symbol of baptism. The inwardness of the second Covenant is contrasted with the externalism of the first Covenant. The SPRINKLING and the WASHING taken together are a description of the process of becoming a Christian, by conversion, i.e. repentance and acceptance of forgiveness, and by baptism.

Let us trust in God to fulfil his promise of eternal life

with him. This is our HOPE and this is the CONFESSION of
faith we made at baptism. But let us think not only of
ourselves but of our neighbours, and busy ourselves in
WORKS of kindness and charity. Notice how in this passage
the distinctive triad of Christian virtues appears: FAITH,
HOPE and LOVE.

25. not forsaking the assembling of ourselves together as the custom of some is

This may simply be a caution against solitary Christianity,
or it may be a general warning against the readers absenting
themselves from church meetings because of fear of persecution. Another possibility is that the readers, if they had
Gnostic leanings, may have felt themselves superior to the
common herd and thought they were able to do without
public worship. If however the readers were Christian Jews
with backward-looking tendencies, as is more likely, this
would suggest that they were ceasing to attend the normal
gatherings of the Church, perhaps even drifting back into
the orbit of the synagogue. The reason for this may have
been persecution, as is suggested later in this chapter, or
disappointment at the non-arrival of the Parousia, to which
reference is made in this verse and in v. 37 (see note), or it
may have been a combination of these with the general
nostalgia for the cut and dried religious rites of Judaism
which seems to have been suggested before.

THE SIN BEYOND PARDON
10.26-31

In the light of what has just been said it would appear
that the next few verses are designed, like those in an earlier
chapter (6.4-6), to put any idea of apostasy to Judaism out
of the readers' minds. Under Mosaic Law, says the Author,
if a man rebelled against God to the extent of denying him

and worshipping meaningless symbols (Deut. 17.2-6; 13.6-10) he was stoned to death. He had stepped outside the Covenant and for that there was no pardon. How much more is this true of the New Covenant. Once a man has come to know God in Christ he is bound to Christ for ever. Christ's death has blotted out his past sins. But that can only happen once in each man's life. Christ has sacrificed himself once and cannot do so again. If the Christian has appropriated his sacrifice once it cannot be repeated. All that he can expect is the Judgement of God and the destruction which as Isaiah said awaits his enemies (Isa. 26.11). To apostatize from Christianity is to trample on the Son of God, to profane the Covenant blood, by treating it as if it were the blood of animals or common men. It is blasphemy against the Spirit of God, and he will exact full retribution (Deut. 32.35-36). 'You cannot play fast and loose with God.'

IN FACE OF DANGER
10.32-39

The last section of chapter 10 is again a parallel to chapter 6. For having denounced apostasy as the unforgivable sin the Author goes on to say, as before, that the situation is not so black as he has painted it. There is every reason for confidence. First the readers had already learned how to suffer, and second they had learned how to rise above the chances and changes of this world. The persecution cannot have been severe as there is no reference to martyrdom (cf. 12.4), but rather to derision and insults. That would seem to rule out the Neronian outbreak in A.D. 64. The SPOILING OF POSSESSIONS suggests not so much judicial confiscation as mob law. The most likely solution seems to be that the Author is referring to the incident in A.D. 49, when the Emperor Claudius issued an edict expelling the

H

Jews from the city of Rome. Suetonius describes the affair thus: 'He drove the Jews from Rome for continually making disturbances at the instigation of Chrestus.'

Allowing for a Roman historian's natural vagueness in dealing with what he doubtless did not exert himself to understand, it is possible that this is a reference to disturbances caused by Christians making propaganda in the synagogues. Judaism was tolerated as a religion in the Empire, provided the Jews kept the peace, but no doubt if rioting occurred the authorities did not stop to distinguish between Christians and Jews, but got rid of the troublesome elements of both parties (cf. Acts 18.2) and punished the rest. It is possible that the readers were the remnant of this original group of Jewish Christians in Rome.

THE PAROUSIA

At all events they are congratulated by the Author on their record on that occasion. They bore their share of sufferings bravely and did not disguise their allegiance. They helped those who were imprisoned and showed a true Christian indifference to the loss of worldly possessions. This in its turn was based on their Christian hope to which they must hold fast with patience, and for the second time in this chapter (cf. v. 25) the Author refers to the Second Coming of Christ.

He quotes Isa. 26.20 and Hab. 2.3-4, which was also quoted by St. Paul (Rom. 1.17; Gal. 3.11). But the Apostle used the words of the prophet to support his doctrine of justification by faith. The Author uses the same words more in the sense that Habakkuk intended, where FAITH meant faithfulness or fidelity, and he goes on in the next chapter to expound this more fully. Meantime he says they must live by faith in the light of the speedy Advent of the Lord. This Messianic reference was not in Habakkuk, whose words have been slightly altered by the Author to make them refer to Christ. This double allusion to the Parousia might suggest that one reason for the inclination of the readers to slip back into Judaism may have been the failure of Christ to appear as was popularly expected. Such an attitude would reflect the concern of the conservative section of Jewish Christians who thought in terms of a speedy return of the Messiah to found a specifically Israelite Kingdom of God (Acts 1.6f.) as opposed to the radical party of which Stephen was the founder and to which the Author belongs, who maintained that first of all the Gospel must be carried to the Gentiles.

XI

THE ROLL OF HONOUR
11.1-40

This famous and fascinating chapter not only provides a useful refresher in Old Testament history but also strikes a fitting and timely note for Christian life to-day. It was written to men who had lost the keen edge of their former conviction. Their religious life had gone stale. In addition to that their world had become a dangerous place. The forces arrayed against them appeared to be overwhelming. Wherever they looked there seemed to be no break in the clouds. To summon them to witness for Christ in the world was to invite them to face even more hazards. It was an adventure into the unknown with no guarantee of a safe return. How much wiser to stay secure among the old familiar ways and to hold fast to the beliefs and practices that had stood the test of time!

As we have seen the Author will have none of this. Christianity is forward-looking and outward-going. The Christian life has to be lived on a minimum of security. It means courting danger and inviting hostility. Ancient habits of thought and action must be superseded by commitment to the living Christ to do his bidding wherever that may lead. But once a man is anchored to him,

> ' Hobgoblin nor foul fiend can daunt his spirit,
> He knows he at the end shall life inherit.'

It is in this sense that the Author pens his great clarion call to venture all for Christ in the sure knowledge that behind the perplexities and turmoil of the world as we know it stands the unchanging Realm of God to which Christ beckons us.

The theme of the chapter is Faith, and it connects up with the last verse of chapter 10, where the Author has defined a Christian as a man who does not shrink from danger and thereby atrophies his spirit, but who lives by his faith and thereby wins his soul. And faith means trusting in God come what may, believing in the truth and reality of his Providence when everything seems to make such a belief crazy. It does not simply mean hoping that things will turn out all right. That is merely humanist optimism. Faith rests on a personal relationship to God, a fellowship with him which takes us out of the here and now at any moment into his Presence. We are in this world but we are at the same time able to enter the Beyond and Hereafter. It is by this experience and certain knowledge that the world and our life are put in their proper perspective, because we see them in the light of eternity. Thus as we look round on the world as we know it, and it was vast and incomprehensible even to first century Christians, our faith tells us that it has not just 'happened', but that behind it is the creative power of God (v. 3). (cf. Rom. 1.20.)

This conviction was what made Israel great, and from vv. 4-40 the Author leads us through the story of the People of God from Abel to the Maccabeans, illustrating from one case after another that these were men who lived by the conviction that the things they saw around them, and the things that happened to them were not God's last word. It is a recital that reminds us at once of that other Roll of Honour, also fittingly associated with Remembrance Day, in Ecclus. 44.

But there is an even closer connection with Stephen's similar review of the heroes of Israel's faith in Acts 7 because of the community of thought behind both. Stephen saw the story of Israel as the story of a nation that had failed in its task of bringing the world back to God despite the pleadings of prophetic voices and the example of their leadership from Abraham onwards. God wanted all men; Israel chose to believe that he wanted only the Jews. The circle to which this letter was addressed within the New Israel seems to have shared Old Israel's reluctance to embark on evangelical enterprise (cf. 5.12), which meant in the first instance to identify themselves openly with the Christian cause in the pagan capital of the Empire, with all that that might mean and had already meant in terms of public contempt, mob violence, loss of property and possibly death. But their Christian duty was plain, and the Author's task is to persuade them, by citing examples, that if they looked back over the history of their own people they would see that it was by the motive power of faith that the greatest of their forefathers had lived and died to the glory of God, and triumphed over the worst that the world could do to them.

4. Abel

The first example, Abel, is unfortunately not impressive. The Author assumes that the reason why Abel's sacrifice was accepted while Cain's was not was that Abel must have had FAITH. Therefore his name lives on. Whatever elements lie behind this story of Genesis 4.1-10, it is difficult to see where faith comes into the picture at all.

5. Enoch

The second example is little better. Enoch's translation is taken to be a proof of his faith, though probably all that is meant by the Genesis reference is that he died young. The Septuagint gives a certain nuance to the Hebrew original (cf. Gen. 5.24) in saying that Enoch 'pleased God' rather than simply WALKED WITH GOD. The Author's point, based on this, is that to please God it is necessary to have faith in him, and such faith is rewarded. Since we cannot take either of these two incidents at its face value, as the Author did, we shall find both of them unconvincing. The readers, however, would no doubt take the point, not because they were more gullible, but because this type of argument was for them conclusive.

7. Noah

With Noah the pattern becomes clearer. Noah built an Ark at the command of God, although at the time there was no indication of the impending Flood. He showed thus that he had FAITH in God despite all appearances to the contrary. By his action he proved that he recognized that the world was wrong and that God was right, thus becoming the kind of man who was in the proper relationship to him.

8. Abraham

It is perhaps inevitable that when the Author is arguing from history he should be more successful with historical figures than mythological ones. Thus the best example so far is Abraham, who at least existed. The reference is to Gen. 12.1f. Abraham is regarded as the perfect prototype because he had such faith in God that he was prepared to leave the security of Ur and venture out into the unknown at his behest. It need not detract from the Author's argument that Abraham's departure may have been connected with the threat of an Elamite invasion. So far as the Author knew from his reading of Scripture, this kind of courageous enterprise, undertaken solely in the conviction that God had called the patriarch to leave the narrow horizon that he knew and go out into the world, trusting only in his Promise, was precisely what Christ wanted from his followers. A further proof of Abraham's faith was that he did not despair when he came to the Promised Land and found it occupied by strangers. He was content to spend his life as a tent-dweller because his faith was in something more enduring than an earthly inheritance, namely the Heavenly City WHOSE BUILDER AND MAKER IS GOD. The

Author likewise takes it to be a proof of faith that Sarah
was able to bear a son at an advanced age. The Old Testament record however suggests derision rather than faith as
Sarah's attitude (Gen. 18).

13-16. In an interpolation, which breaks the recital, the
Author asserts that all these nomadic patriarchs were content
to have no fixed foothold on earth, because they recognized
that here they were STRANGERS AND PILGRIMS, while cherish-
ing in their hearts the hope of the Heavenly City which they
have now inherited. It may well be that here we have an
echo of Jesus' words in Mark 12.26-27, where he speaks of
the patriarchs as now living with God. In both cases the
thought is that the lives of the patriarchs were anchored in
God, which is faith, and because of that they are now with
him for ever. It is not difficult to see the relevance of these
words for the situation of the Jewish Christians in Rome.

17-19. Returning to ABRAHAM the Author sees the supreme
example of his faith in his readiness to sacrifice his son
Isaac in response to what he believed to be the will of God.
Indeed the Author uses the perfect tense ('has offered up')
to indicate that in God's sight the action was as good as
done (Gen. 22.1-19). Abraham's faith was so great that
though Isaac was his only son, and God had promised
Abraham that his offspring would grow into a great nation,
he believed that God was capable of raising Isaac from the
dead. This, adds the Author in parenthesis, is a prefigura-
tion of the Resurrection of Christ. St. Augustine went
further with his symbolism and saw in the faggots the Cross,
and, in the ram caught in the thicket, Christ wearing the
Crown of Thorns.

20. Isaac

Little is said of Isaac since there appears to be little that
can be said of him. Abraham and Jacob are much more

colourful personalities. Isaac's faith is exemplified in that he blessed his sons in terms that showed his belief in God's promise to Abraham. The Author's memory is again playing him tricks, since it was only Jacob who was blessed. What Isaac said to Esau could hardly be called a blessing (Gen. 27).

21. Jacob

Jacob handed on the blessing to his grandchildren in a like faith (Gen. 48.9f.). The reference to his bowing in prayer UPON THE TOP OF HIS STAFF, which properly belongs to another incident (Gen. 47.31), should be compared with the Old Testament text which says that Jacob BOWED HIM-SELF UPON THE BED'S HEAD. The reason for the discrepancy is that Hebrew was originally written without vowels. When the translators of the Septuagint found the consonants MTTH they concluded that it was MATTEH, which is a 'staff', and rendered it into Greek accordingly. Several centuries later when vowels were added to the Hebrew text it appeared that the original word had been MITTAH, a 'bed'. The author reproduces the Septuagint while our R.V. reproduces the Hebrew.

22. Joseph

All these patriarchs exhibited the quality which the Author commended by believing in something which they could not see, and which seemed at the time well nigh impossible, namely the growth and establishment of the People of God. Joseph's faith was even more notable in that before there was any oppression of the Israelites in Egypt he foresaw the Exodus and made arrangements for his mummified body to be taken to the Land of the Promise (Gen. 50.24f.).

23-29. Moses

The Author comes now to the Exodus itself, and sees in the life of Moses several moments of deep significance, as illustrations of faith. His parents exemplified it by defying the king's orders (Ex. 2.1f.), although Calvin thought their abandonment of Moses in the bulrushes was rather an example of collapse of faith. The Author did not have Calvin's logical mind.

Moses himself however showed his faith by refusing to be recognized as the son of Pharaoh's daughter and by disdaining high office in the Egyptian court. This seems to be the most probable meaning of THE PLEASURES OF SIN. The Old Testament knows nothing of this, but there is a story in Josephus of the infant Moses throwing Pharaoh's crown upon the floor. In maintaining his Hebrew origins and pledging himself to a People of God, which did not then seem possible, he chose to share the REPROACH OF CHRIST. The Author comments that the People of God always suffer unjustly and implies that Christ, the Messiah who represented the People of God, was therefore already suffering with Israel in Egypt. Moses in identifying himself with Israel was looking by faith beyond the REPROACH to the REWARD (cf. I Cor. 4.10). It may be that in the Author's mind is the parallel between on the one hand Moses rejecting the TREASURES OF EGYPT and choosing THE REPROACH OF CHRIST, and on the other, the readers of this letter sighing for the privileges of Judaism, which was a *religio licita*, and shrinking from the hazards of publicly confessing themselves to be Christians. His question in that case would no doubt be: Moses threw in his lot with Christ, what about you?

The flight to Midian (Ex. 2.11f.), which the Old Testament ascribes to fear of Pharaoh, is taken to be a further example of faith. The Author may however have meant that Moses showed his faith by recognizing that what seemed to be the end of his high hopes was in fact a sign that he must wait until God's time was ripe. At all events what sustained Moses was that above the visible king he could see by faith the invisible King. In the same spirit he celebrated the

Passover because he believed that God had a future for his People, and by trusting in him led Israel across the Red Sea. The Egyptians who tried to follow were drowned because of their lack of faith.

30-31. Rahab

The walls of Jericho fell because of the faith of the invaders, aided, as archaeologists tell us, by an earthquake, while Rahab, who assisted the Israelite spies, saved herself from death by her faith, which she evidenced by believing in the triumph of the God of Israel (Josh. 2.1f.).

32-38. GIDEON TO THE MACCABEANS

The Author, no doubt rightly concluding that such a detailed progress through the history of Israel would be beyond the scope of his letter, proceeds now to summarize his Roll of Honour. He specifies Gideon (Judg. 6-8), Barak (Judg. 4-5), Samson (Judg. 13-16), Jephthah (Judg. 11-12), from the period before the monarchy, as well as David, Samuel and the Prophets. What particular evidence of their faith he had in mind we cannot say. The first four are not examples that would naturally have come to mind as being of the same calibre as David, Samuel and the Prophets, but according to their lights they were men who lived by their faith in Yahweh. Then, giving up the attempt to name the heroes of faith further, he proceeds to catalogue some of their achievements. No doubt the allusions were clear enough to the readers, though the best we can do now is to guess at most of them. By their faith they conquered kingdoms, like Joshua and David; administered justice, like Solomon (I Kings 3.16-28); stopped the mouths of lions, like Daniel (Dan. 6); quenched the power of fire, like the Three Men in the Fiery Furnace (Dan. 3); escaped the edge of the sword, like Jeremiah (26) or Elijah (I Kings 19). Their weakness was turned to strength, like Samson (Judg. 16.28-30), Hezekiah (II Kings 20), or Judith (13); they were valiant

in battle, they routed their enemies. Some were even raised
from the dead, like the sons of the widow of Zarephath and
the Shunammite (I Kings 17.8-24; II Kings 4.18-37), or the
heroic brothers of the Maccabean rebellion (II Macc. 7.29).

But all the men of faith in Israel's story did not receive
their reward on earth. Many of them chose death rather
than betray their Lord. Yet it was their faith that enabled
them to endure whatever ills the world chose to inflict on
them. They were beaten, chained and imprisoned. Some
were stoned, like Zechariah (II Chron. 24.21), or sawn in
two as was said to have been Isaiah's fate in the evil reign
of Manasseh. Others were broken on the wheel (TORTURED)
like Eleazar (II Macc. 6.18f.). (The word translated as
TEMPTED in the R.V. is probably a scribal error and should
possibly mean ' burned '). Many more were forced to seek
refuge in mountains and caves as happened during the
persecution of Antiochus Epiphanes in the second century
B.C.

39-40. no vain sacrifice

These were men of faith who died apparently to no purpose. Yet their sacrifice was not in vain, for God had a
greater purpose for them, namely that they should be incor-
porated in his People in Messiah's Realm. The promise was
not fulfilled under the Old Covenant, but their reward was
only delayed. It was God's will that the fulfilment of Israel's
history and the blessings of the Messianic Age should be
deferred until now, but in it the heroes of faith under the
old régime would share with Christian men of faith in the
glory of God's eternal Kingdom.

XII

THE CHRISTIAN RACE
12.1-3

Once again the Author has returned to the thought that Christ was present with Israel throughout its history. The panorama of faith in chapter 11 has been seen as Israel's response to Christ which is now fulfilled and rewarded. In the first three verses of chapter 12, which properly form a conclusion to the previous chapter, he applies the point he has been making to his readers. The Christian life is a RACE to be run by all of us. If we are to reach the tape we must be dressed for the part. No athlete can run in his everyday clothes. Nor can we run the Christian race unless we have first got rid of everything that would hinder us, the sins that cling to us and keep us back. The Author does not mean our 'besetting sin', though the R.V. would suggest that. It is rather any failing of mind or body that weakens our performance. In the case of his readers it was their nostalgic backward looks to the cut and dried certainties of their old faith.

It is a race we must run steadily (with PATIENCE) encouraged by the example of the heroes of FAITH of whom we have just been reminded, and who now like a CLOUD OF WITNESSES line the way to the winning post cheering us on. At the post is Christ himself, the supreme example of faith and our chief encouragement. It is on him that our eyes must be fixed and our minds bent as we run towards him, as it was by looking towards him that the saints of Israel won the race in their day. For the race has been run before us by Jesus the Leader and Captain of faith (AUTHOR) and its perfect embodiment (PERFECTER). In order to reach the JOY that lay ahead of him, which also awaits us, he disregarded the indignity of the Cross and bore its pain, and now awaits us at God's side. Whatever obstacles lie in our way, none can be greater than he has overcome. Therefore let us think constantly of him and revive our flagging spirits with the recollection of what he had to endure from the evil that is in mankind.

It is likely that AGAINST THEMSELVES is more correct than the marginal AGAINST HIMSELF. The latter would be a reference to Calvary and would not add much to what has been said, the former would mean that those who sinned against Jesus sinned against themselves, or against their better selves, or it might refer to the conflicting evidence of the witnesses at his trial.

RESISTANCE UNTO BLOOD
12.4

This is an important point in deciding the date of the epistle. There have been two references already to persecution. Both of them (6.9-10 and 10.32-34) indicate an earlier period in the lives of the readers when they suffered hardship and violence for the gospel's sake. The present reference, and the whole undertone of the epistle, suggest that once again they are being called on to witness for their faith. This time, however, it appears that martyrdom itself is now more than a remote possibility. The words used, YE HAVE NOT YET RESISTED UNTO BLOOD do not however settle the historical question beyond dispute. Whatever other martyrs there had been (cf. 13.7), blood was certainly shed copiously in A.D. 64, when Nero in his madness sought to rid himself of a troublesome element in society by blaming the Great Fire of Rome upon the Christians. At that time, as Tacitus tells us, Christians were covered with animal skins and then torn to pieces by dogs, crucified round the royal gardens, or made into human torches to illuminate the ghastly scene after nightfall, while the crazed Emperor dashed wildly round the arena dressed as a charioteer.

If the persecution of FORMER DAYS referred to in 6.9-10 and 10.32-34 (see note) took place at the time of the expulsion of Jews and Christians from Rome in A.D. 49 under Claudius, the time of writing this epistle must be somewhere between that date and A.D. 64. Most probably it would be nearer 64 than 49 since martyrdom loomed large in the foreground. If there were signs of serious trouble impending for Christians say in about A.D. 60, this would account for the readers reflecting, in addition to the other attractions of the Jewish religion, on the considerable advantage of living under the shelter of a faith which enjoyed the tolerance of the State.

On the other hand the Author's words could mean: ' you have not yet shed blood ' instead of 'you have not yet *had* to shed blood '. This would suggest that martyrdom had already taken place but that the particular group to which the Author was writing had avoided it by hiding behind the synagogue. The date of the letter would therefore be A.D. 64 or shortly after. Such a situation would be in harmony with the other references in this letter to the ultra-Jewish interest of the readers, but it is more than likely, if this were the case, that the Author's language would have been vitriolic, instead of which he suggests that it is rather a case of a danger to be avoided than a fact to be condemned. Further it would be difficult for Jewish Christians to plead their allegiance to the Jewish faith in face of the hatred with which apostates from Judaism were regarded by their countrymen, some of whom would certainly have taken delight in informing against them.

There is, of course, a third possibility, namely that this letter was written long after A.D. 64 to those who during Nero's persecution had been mere children, and had therefore never been faced with martyrdom. That would leave us the difficulty of identifying the persecution of 10.32-34, and we should have to classify it as a bloodless outbreak sometime after Nero and otherwise unknown. On the other hand, the absorption with Jewish ritual suggests that the Temple, which was destroyed in A.D. 70, was still a force to be reckoned with, and exerted a strong fascination for ex-Jews. Also, as has been suggested, the marked emphasis in chapter 3 on the forty years after the Exodus lends weight to the placing of the date of the epistle early in the sixties. This would be approaching forty years after the Second Exodus which began in A.D. 26 with the Baptism of Jesus.

GOD'S DISCIPLINE
12.5-11

The Author now reminds his readers of the words of **Prov.** 3.11-12, in which God tells us that suffering is a wholesome discipline and that it is proof that we are his own children. For whom he loves he chastens. It is part of our spiritual education. We must therefore neither treat our sufferings as if they did not matter, nor collapse under them. Every human father disciplines his children, and the Author plainly agrees that to spare the rod is to spoil the child. To escape such discipline is no mark of God's favour, but rather an indication that we are no sons of his. Human fathers are fallible mortals and their chastisement is a momentary affair. God on the other hand in disciplining us does it for our eternal good. Unpleasant it may well be at the time, but its ultimate aim and result is the strengthening of our moral fibre. Note the reference in v. 9 to the universal Fatherhood of God (cf. 2.11).

WEAKER BRETHREN
12.12-17

In every Christian community exposed to attack from outside there are always weaker brethren who succumb more easily than the rest. These need to be helped by the more robust elements. The Author seems to be thinking again of the Christian race, because Isa. 35.3 is quoted in support of lending a hand to those who need it most. We must make the path straight for them, removing stumbling blocks, so that those already lame should not completely dislocate their joints, but find that on a smooth road their lameness disappears and they too reach the finishing post sound in wind and limb (vv. 12-13).

We must try to agree with one another yet aim at having the 'clean hands' and 'pure heart' without which no man will be fit to face his Maker at the Day of Judgement. Even one bad character like Esau may contaminate the rest.

16. Esau

It is perhaps surprising at first glance that Esau should be singled out as the prime example of an evil influence in the community. His wily brother Jacob is, according to the record, much less attractive. Esau was, however, traditionally the progenitor of the hated Edomites (Gen. 36.1) and their infamies, including those of the Herods, attached themselves to their ancestor. Besides, to a race which took the matter of its birthright as People of God so seriously, a man who tossed aside his inheritance as a thing of no value for the sake of the satisfaction of a momentary appetite was beyond forgiveness. In such a case there was no possibility of repentance for all his tears (Gen. 25.33; 27.30-40).

The point of introducing Esau in this context is that he was a man of no FAITH. He distrusted God's promise to

Abraham and his heirs. He himself was in the direct line
of descent, yet he cast away the right to be the Father of
Israel, which then passed to his brother, in return for an
ephemeral pleasure. Some in the little community in Rome
were likewise in danger of throwing away their birthright,
the hope of eternal life in Christ, by thinking of the safety
of their skins instead of the salvation of their souls. The
word FORNICATOR has therefore no physical connotation
here.

THE HEAVENLY ZION
12.18-24

The Author now bursts into a magnificent piece of
imaginative writing, one of the purple passages of the New
Testament, and indeed of the whole Bible. It is the last
great theme of the epistle. In measured cadences and with
a solemnity and authority that remind us of the great
prophets, he contrasts Judaism and Christianity in terms
of their ability to bring men face to face with God. The
gloom and fearfulness of life under the Old Covenant is
poetically described in terms of the giving of the Law at
Mount Sinai, while the light and liberation that the Gospel
brings are represented by a picture of the heavenly Mount
Zion.

SINAI

The Old Covenant, inaugurated by the giving of the Law
on Sinai, was heralded by fire, cloud and storm, by an
uncanny trumpet blast and an unearthly voice. The selec-
tion of these features from the Old Testament story conveys
to the full the atmosphere of darkness and terror as the
Author intends (Ex. 19; Deut. 5.22f.). So awful was the voice
of God that the people besought Moses to speak to him on
their behalf. So terrifying was the mountain itself that it

was death to touch it (Ex. 19.12-13). The tabu was on it because Yahweh was there. To come in contact with him or even to approach him was fatal. This forbidding and paralysing relationship was further reflected in the gloomy rigours of the Law both on its moral and ritual side. Thus were God and man kept apart and life was savourless and joyless.

ZION

However well the psalmists may have bridged this gulf and delighted in their communion with God, it was nevertheless a true picture of what Pharisee and Priest had made of the Covenant. 'But, look,' cries the Author, 'at the glories of the New Age', and with every word he strikes a nail into the coffin of the old régime. Again it is in symbolic language that the picture is conveyed—the Heavenly City, the angelic host, the communion of Saints, the Judge and the Mediator. But the total effect is one of life and light, of fellowship and reconciliation with God, of liberation from fear and exaltation of spirit. When we would worship God it is to no sombre Sinai that we as Christians turn our eyes, only to shrink back in terror from his Presence, but to the heights of heaven, the Holy City on high, where enthroned amid the adoring throng sit the Judge whom we know as Father, and the Son through whom we have forgiveness.

THE NEW JERUSALEM

Mount Zion, the hill on which Jerusalem was built, is seen as the mere shadow of the Heavenly City. Myriads of angels, the messengers and ministers of God, according to the belief of the times, are described as gathered in festal array. With them are the firstborn of Christ, who have finished the course and whose names are written in heaven (Rev. 21.27). With them too are the spirits of the saints of whom we have been hearing, the faithful men of Israel who have now received their reward.   God reigns supreme, the Judge of all men's hearts, with Jesus through whom we may have part in this triumphal scene, and whose sacrifice has made it possible.   Abel's blood under the Old Covenant cried out for vengeance (Gen. 4.10), Jesus' blood proclaims forgiveness.

This then is the dimension in which the Christian lives by faith, a member of the Church in heaven as well as the Church on earth.   This is the inheritance which awaits him, the fulfilment of the Promise, which he can however share in part here and now, since Christ has opened up the way.

There is no doubt that each point in this piece of imagery was consciously made with reference to the readers of the epistle.   It is a composite picture of the supersession by something better and more enduring of all that they tended to cling to.   Jerusalem, dear as it was to them, was but a dim reflection of the City they could now claim as their own. The angels who traditionally delivered the Law to Israel were now replaced by the Angels of the Presence.   Israel, the firstborn child of God, had been superseded by the Church of the firstborn of Christ.   The Old Covenant with its blood ritual had given place to a New Covenant sealed in the blood of Jesus.

THE VOICE OF GOD
12.25-29

God has now spoken for a second time, and we disregard his voice at our peril.   When he spoke before it was in the words of the Ten Commandments, and yet though Israel trembled at the sound of his voice they disobeyed him and were punished.   We shall certainly not escape if we do not heed him now when he speaks from heaven.   Then his voice shook the earth (Ex. 19.18), although in the Greek version which the Author used it was the people who trembled. Next time, however, heaven and earth will quake. These words from Haggai 2.6 are of course referred by the Author to the end of all things. Yet, he goes on, this will not affect the Church of Christ because it belongs by nature to a realm that is changeless. Let us therefore give thanks to God (not 'have grace') and serve him with fitting REVERENCE AND AWE. We must not presume on his goodness for he is a CONSUMING FIRE (Deut. 4.24).

The Author would say to us, in this practical application of the preceding paragraph, that we as Christians have been granted through Christ the inestimable privilege of a direct aproach to God. But let us beware lest we treat this privilege lightly. In a changing world let us hold fast to the unchanging verities and remember above all that to worship God is the supreme activity of man. Let us be warned by Israel's example. By refusing to listen to the word that God spoke through Moses, they lost the Promised Land. Likewise we shall lose the true Promised Land, which is eternal communion with God, if we do not listen to the word he has now spoken in Christ.

XIII

CHRISTIAN CONDUCT
13.1-8

The last chapter of the epistle begins with various injunctions of an ethical nature. The Author exhorts his readers to brotherly LOVE. It was in fact one of the best advertisements for the Church in its early days that the Christian charity of its members was such as to impress and attract pagan observers. Nothing like it existed anywhere else (cf. I Thess. 1.8). Christian hospitality is also commended. Not only were the inns indifferent or bad, but in a time of persecution the problem of refugees would become acute. The allusion to entertaining ANGELS UNAWARES is to Gen. 18. There are those who have been imprisoned for their faith. Care of them is also a Christian duty. So likewise is concern for those who are EVIL ENTREATED, which may mean either illness or hardship.

There is little reference in this letter to sexual vice which is next mentioned. The pagan world was sex-ridden. Not only was sacramental prostitution a feature of religious practice, but the moral standards of the theatre, and of public and private life generally, had at this time reached a deplorably low level. The tone was set by the profligacies and debaucheries of the Caesars. In such a cesspool, the Jews formed an island of moral rectitude. Whatever their failings in the direction of spiritual arrogance and self-righteousness, the wholesomeness of their home life and their probity of character attracted attention and, on the part of the more responsible pagans, respect. Christian congregations culled from a Gentile background, like the Church at Corinth (cf. I Cor. 5), sometimes found it extremely difficult to adapt themselves to the new standards of personal relationships that the Gospel demanded. The fact that this aspect of behaviour is so little mentioned in this letter argues for the Jewish upbringing of the readers.

In the same breath almost the Author warns against LOVE OF MONEY. This was often taken together with sexual licence as constituting a twin danger in the Christian life. Not only did it lead to unlovely traits of character, but also it indicated a lack of faith in Providence. Here it is the latter point which is stressed with two Old Testament quotations (Josh. 1.5; Ps. 118.6), which seems to suggest that the readers had lost or might lose what wealth they had through persecution, and encourages them to put their trust in heaven rather than in riches.

The readers are reminded of the founders of their Church, names that are now unknown, who brought the Gospel to Rome. From what is said, it appears that they had died a martyr's death. Follow the example of their faith, says the Author, and remember that though they are dead Jesus Christ remains, and he gives the same strength, hope and courage to you now as he gave to them, yes, and will go on doing so to his people for ever. In view of the Author's estimate of Jesus, however, we ought properly to think in terms of a more profound interpretation. 'The Yesterday of Jesus Christ,' he would say, 'does not merely extend back to the lifetime of the founders of the local Church nor indeed to his own life on earth, but to his eternal pre-existence with the Father, and his presence in Israel throughout the preparation for his coming.' This is the Christ whom we know to-day and whom we shall know more fully hereafter.

GO FORTH
13.9-14

Sometimes at the end of a Beethoven sonata or symphony,

when the theme seems to have been exhausted and the work brought to a close, a sudden startling crescendo reminds us that the master is still with us and that he has a final trump card to play. This striking and controversial passage, coming as it does amid a collection of fairly ordinary ethical precepts, after the main subject of the epistle has been dealt with, provides a perfect analogy. It not only recapitulates the theme but takes us up to what may well be regarded as its climax.

GRACE NOT MEATS

The main problem is to know what the Author meant by MEATS and what he meant by ALTAR, and the answer depends to some extent on what conclusions we have already come to about the epistle in general. Thus if we think on other grounds that the letter is addressed to a community which harboured the same eccentric notions of Christianity as the Church of Colossae, we shall take the Author's point about MEATS to be concerned with the Gnostic idea that since all matter is evil the flesh must be mortified, and that therefore asceticism, including abstention from food, is a Christian virtue. The difficulty here would be that the Author seems to be speaking in v. 9 of fortifying ourselves with grace, and the parallel to that in the following verse would be a reference to body-building rather than to body-wasting.

PAGAN MEATS?

If on the other hand, like some commentators, we think that the Author was addressing a group with a pagan background, whose danger was that of incorporating features of pagan religion into Christianity, we should probably regard the reference as applying to the sacramental and sacrificial meats of the Mystery Religions. Most meat which could be purchased in a city of the Roman Empire had been dedicated to some pagan god or other, and the basic superstition was that by eating such flesh one appropriated the power of the deity in whose honour it had been sacrificed. St. Paul had to deal with this problem in his letter to Corinth (I Cor. 8 and 10). It presented a danger in such circles of infiltrating idolatry into Christian practice. This would however be difficult to fit in with other references in the epistle.

EUCHARISTIC MEATS?

Some scholars incline to the view that the passage concerns what the Author feels to be a wrong attitude towards the Eucharist, and that the readers seem to regard the elements as in fact the body and blood of Christ in a material sense. Yet again the belief has been expressed that the point of the passage lies in a contrast between the Christian altar on which the sacrament of Holy Communion is celebrated, and the Jewish equivalent.

There is, however, no real indication that the Author is thinking of the sacrament of Holy Communion at all. Indeed one of the marked features of this letter is that there is no reference to the chief Christian sacrament even where we should have expected it (e.g. 6.1-2: see note). That would seem to suggest not that we should force at all costs some such reference into the letter by treating a passage like this as eucharistic, but that we should recognize that in the Author's view it has not entered the sphere of his argument. There is still less reason to think that his silence indicates disapproval. The Eucharist was entrenched in Christian belief and practice from the beginning, but we should not omit to note that it was not mentioned in such an irreproachable work as the Epistle to the Romans.

THE JEWISH ALTAR

If, on the other hand, we take this paragraph to be related to the general situation envisaged in the preceding chapters, it not only fits in admirably with the main theme of the letter but leaves fewer question marks behind individual points of

interpretation than any other solution. Let us then assume
that the MEATS referred to are the ritual food laws of
Judaism already mentioned (see note on 9.10), and which
would form part of the attraction of the old *régime* for
Jewish Christians who were beginning to wonder, partly
under the threat of persecution, whether there was not more
to be said for the cut and dried religious life on which they
had been reared than this dangerous uncertain adventure,
this life on a knife edge, which constituted Christianity.

The Author then having reminded his readers (v. 8) of the
permanent security offered by a life of allegiance to Christ,
goes on to warn them against being attracted to various
extraneous ideas which have nothing to do with Christianity
(v. 9). Jesus Christ is the source of all spiritual nourishment. It is his GRACE alone that makes life wholesome and
sound. Observance of the Jewish laws of eating certain
things that were held to be permissible and abstaining from
others because they were ritually 'unclean', laws which
derived from and were associated with the sacrificial rites
of the Temple, could never build up a religious life worth
having, however ancient and hallowed the practice might be.
It had never done so in the past and could not do so now.
This was not what they had been taught by the founders of
their Church (v. 7).

WITHIN THE CAMP

The next problem is to ascertain what the Author means
by ALTAR in this particular context. The clue lies in vv.
11-12 in the phrases WITHOUT THE CAMP and WITHOUT THE
GATE. There, clearly, a parallel is being drawn between
Jesus' death outside the walls of Jerusalem, the normal place
of execution, and that part of the ritual on the Day of Atonement which enjoined that the body of the sacrificial animal
should be burned outside the CAMP, i.e. in the desert days
the tents of the People of God grouped round his Tabernacle.
This picture of the tribes of Israel grouped round the Tent

of the Lord is however rather a priestly ideal than a historic
fact. The evidence of Exodus (e.g. 33.7) is that the Tent of
Meeting was pitched well away from the camp.

The practice was that in the case of regular sacrifices
(peace-offerings) made by ordinary worshippers to celebrate
some occasion, part of the animal was consumed by the
persons making the offering and part by the priests. In the
case of ordinary sin-offerings by individual Jews the flesh of
the animals was consumed only by priests on account of its
holiness (Lev. 6.26). But on the Day of Atonement so
sacred was the rite that, when the blood of the animals had
been sprinkled on the Mercy-seat as a token of reconciliation, the carcasses were not consumed at all, but were taken
outside the 'camp', i.e. to a remote spot, and there ceremonially burned (Lev. 16.27).

The point which the Author is making is therefore that
there is no parallel between the Jewish belief that the flesh
of animals ritually sacrificed on the ALTAR benefited the
worshipper in some way, and what Christians mean by their
ALTAR. The true parallel is between the sacrifice of Christ
and the ritual of the Day of Atonement. Our altar is
different in kind from that of the Temple. It has nothing
at all to do with a levitical priesthood (WHICH SERVE THE
TABERNACLE) because it consists of a sacrifice that cannot be
eaten. As priests they may partake of the ordinary
sacrificial food of the Temple, but of the special sin-offerings
they may not partake (Lev. 4.1f.). The High Priest himself
may not consume a morsel of the offerings on the Day of
Atonement. On that Day the victims, after their blood has
effected the Atonement, are taken out of the precincts of the
Temple. Likewise Jesus, to reconcile men with God,
suffered outside Jerusalem and all that it represented. His
offering was made beyond Temple, Law and Cultus. Indeed
he was thrust beyond the walls of the Holy City by the Jews
themselves and there executed like a felon under the curse
of the Law (Deut. 21.23). Ritual, priesthood, sacrifices, food

laws, these are things which belong within the camp, within the gate. They are the narrow concern of Old Israel. Our altar is outside the camp, outside the gate.

THE CHRISTIAN ALTAR

What then is the Christian altar? As can be seen by a careful examination of the Author's compressed thought here, there is no suggestion of identifying the sacrificial animals of the Day of Atonement with Jesus. The parallel is conceived in general terms. The animal sacrifices were designed to effect at-one-ment which they failed to do. The blood of Jesus had done this. But we cannot press the analogy closer, for in that case the equivalent of Jesus offering himself on the Cross would be the burning of the animals' carcasses outside the camp and not the offering of their lives beside the Temple altar.

The answer is probably that the Author was content to paint his picture in a few deft suggestive strokes and did not aim at precise definition. Clearly the Christian altar has here nothing to do with the sacrament of Holy Communion. Is it then the Cross? This was certainly the altar on which Jesus gave himself, but in this passage the contrast is between the Christian altar and the Jewish Tabernacle. If we therefore pursue the general parallel between the Day of Atonement and the Sacrifice which supersedes it we should have to say that the comparable moment of the Day was the sprinkling of the Mercy-seat with the blood of Atonement. The Christian altar would therefore be the heavenly Mercy-seat where Jesus intercedes for men and brings them to God. The Christian altar is thus of a different order. Its sacrifice made once for all was not material but spiritual, and the Author will go on to say (v. 15) that our sacrifices in response must be the spiritual offerings of praise and prayer.

WITHOUT THE CAMP

Meantime he strikes the note which is perhaps determin-

ative in the whole epistle. LET US THEREFORE GO FORTH
UNTO HIM WITHOUT THE CAMP. Our call as Christians is not
to remain within the security of past tradition, as was the
wish of the readers, but to go out to Jesus who, by dying
outside the exclusive orbit of Israel opened the way for all
nations to come to God through him. The call is to follow
him in the spirit of Abraham, not knowing where the path
will lead, but, like Abraham, confident that this world is
not our permament dwelling since we seek the heavenly
CITY WHICH IS TO COME. As we journey towards our goal
we are called to BEAR THE REPROACH of Christ, to share the
obloquy, antagonism and suffering which he endured.

Particularly to his readers the Author says: Jesus has by
being crucified OUTSIDE THE CAMP been thrust beyond the
pale of Judaism. That should be enough for his followers.
Their place is with him there. It is not by backward looks
to the comforts of Judaism, not by nostalgic yearning for
Jerusalem, its Temple, and all that they stand for, not by
timorous retreat into the safety of the synagogue, but in going
out and taking their place beside the crucified Christ in the
midst of a hostile world, and if need be by dying his death,
that their true Christian vocation lies. This was the essence
of the faith of their fathers, the heroes of Israel who fixed
their eyes on no earthly security but on the heavenly City
of the Promise, and this was the faith that had been taught
them by their founders and leaders.

13.15-25

A FINAL BLESSING

Unlike their Jewish kinsmen, for the readers the once-only
sacrifice of Christ was enough. It enabled them, since he
had made it possible for them, to offer to God the worship
that was his due. The Author sees this constantly as the
supreme duty and privilege of men. It is a SACRIFICE OF

PRAISE, a recognition CONTINUALLY of the goodness of God. Another kind of sacrifice which God welcomes is that of good works and charity. COMMUNICATE here means 'share with others '.

The readers are urged to OBEY their leaders, remembering their high sense of responsibility. The Author invites their prayers, and suggests by his words that he stands in a special relationship to the community to which he is writing, perhaps as one of its leaders himself. He is however absent from them for a spell—for what reason we do not know—and he is the more anxious to return to them in that he suspects that what he has just been saying will not be universally well received. His conscience is however clear. All that he has written has been from a sincere concern for the truth.

Now comes a benediction. God is described as he who alone gives men inward peace. Men can now have this peace since the sacrifice of Christ has taken away the burden of guilt and the power of God, WORKING IN US, helps us to do his will which is the only way to maintain inward peace. Jesus is described, in the language of Isa. 63.11 in the Greek version, as the SHEPHERD OF THE SHEEP (cf. John 10.11f.). God has raised him FROM THE DEAD. This is the only reference in the epistle to the Resurrection of Christ. The Author's emphasis throughout has been as we have seen on the death of Christ and the exalted Christ. Since he has made so much of the symbol of the High Priest passing beyond the Veil he has had no occasion to dwell on the intervening moment between the Cross and the right hand of God. Unlike St. Paul the theology of the Author does not lay stress on a mystical union with Christ, whereby we repeat his Death and Resurrection in our own experience by dying to our past life and rising again to new life with him. Here Jesus is pictured as passing from death into the Presence of God, presenting his self-offering, to reign with him as the Shepherd of all his People in the new and eternal relationship which his sacrifice made possible.

The Author concludes by asking his readers to read his letter with patience and understanding, since in so small a compass many points, some of them unacceptable, could only be briefly dealt with. He hopes to see them in company with Timothy, presumably the travelling companion of St. Paul, who appears to have been released from prison, although the words may also simply mean that he has already set out towards them. Probably this mention of Timothy was a strong reason for the ascription of the authorship of Hebrews to the Apostle.

The final salutation would suggest that the letter is addressed to a group within a larger community. This latter is described as ALL THE SAINTS. Further it seems that the officials of the larger community are not included in the addressees.

Of the various possible meanings of the message from the ' Italians ', two seem more likely than the rest. Either Italian Christians living abroad wish to send a message to their friends at home, or Italians living overseas wish to greet some of their fellow exiles elsewhere in the Empire. The former explanation would seem to fit in best with the evidence of the letter as a whole. In this case the previous verses would bear out the suggestion that the letter was addressed to one of the house-churches in Rome (cf. Rom. 16.5, 14, 15), where a small group of Jewish Christians meeting there were tending to separate themselves from the rest of the Christian community, and were showing certain symptoms which disturbed the Author, who seems to have been one of their leading members himself, although temporarily absent. This is as clear a picture as we can get of the background of the letter, although none of it can be taken as certain.

The closing blessing is one frequently used in the New Testament, although shorter than most Pauline benedictions. AMEN is added, since the epistle would be read aloud in the liturgy.